CW01401435

Macbeth
Revision Guide for GCSE
Lynda Nicholson

Series Editor: Nicola Walsh

Firestone Books' no-nonsense guides have all you need
to do brilliantly at your English Literature GCSE

firestonebooks.com

Macbeth
Revision Guide for GCSE
Lynda Nicholson

Series Editor: Nicola Walsh

Text © Lynda Nicholson
Revision and Exam Help © Nicola Walsh

Cover © XL Book Cover Design
xlbookcoverdesign.co.uk

2021 Edition

ISBN-13: 978-1909608269

Published by Firestone Books

firestonebooks.com

You can stay up to date by following Firestone Books on Facebook and Twitter, or subscribing to our fabulous newsletter.

~ CONTENTS ~

Background Information

The Play – Summary and Analysis

Characters

Themes

Form, Structure and Language

Key Quotations and Glossary

Revision and Exam Help

Our fabulous new revision guides are out now!

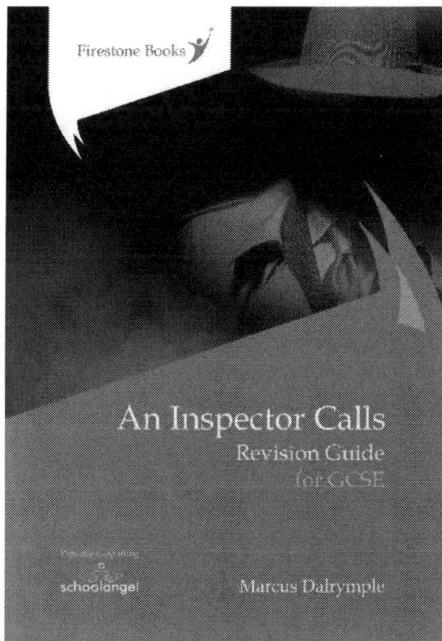

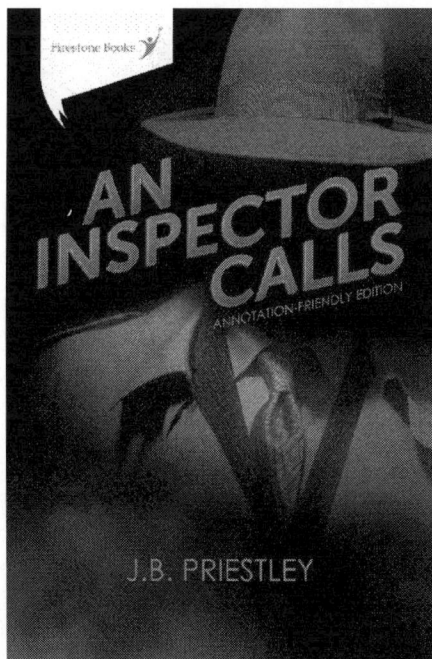

~ BACKGROUND INFORMATION ~

William Shakespeare's Life

William Shakespeare was born in 1564 in Stratford-upon-Avon. His father, John Shakespeare, was a well-off glovemaker, who owned a property in Stratford-upon-Avon. His mother, Mary Arden, was the daughter of a successful farmer. John and Mary Shakespeare had eight children and William was the eldest. During Shakespeare's childhood, Stratford was often a place where travelling groups of actors would visit and perform plays. This may have inspired his interest in writing and he became passionate about pursuing a career in writing plays. This was a risky career as writing and performing plays demanded a patron (someone who would sponsor a play and pay the wages of the performers). If plays were disliked or did not appeal to a patron, then the play would not be performed and, therefore, the actors and playwright would not be paid. The period between 1585 and 1592 was known as the 'lost years', as there is very little information on Shakespeare's life during this time, probably due to a lack of interest in Shakespeare as he was not famous. Although his plays and verses are widely known throughout the world and studied enthusiastically, parts of Shakespeare's personal life are more private and there is little documented about his life and family. He was married at eighteen to Anne Hathaway and they had three children, although his son, Hamnet, died young.

Later Life

Shakespeare began writing seriously when he moved from Stratford-upon-Avon to London around 1592. He realised that one way he could make a living was to write about subjects and events in history. Shakespeare's plays began to become well-known and he was acknowledged as a popular playwright who was able to provide the audience with entertaining and thought-provoking plays. His plays were often about revenge, hate and tragedy. Later, Shakespeare developed his work by writing more about comedy and love. These plays proved just as popular as the revenge and tragedy plays. Also, some of the wealthier citizens appeared to enjoy historical drama and his name began to be known at the court of Queen Elizabeth. Her audience and royal courtiers enjoyed the plays and word spread to influential lords who often asked him to entertain their guests with some of his plays.

As his popularity grew, he was able to form his own company of all-male actors: 'The Lord Chamberlain's Men'. In 1576 the first London theatre was built and a short time later 'The Globe' theatre was erected. This was a purpose-built theatre and made it much easier for actors to perform their plays.

Shakespeare was a popular writer and began to accumulate a large amount of wealth, which meant he was able to buy property in Stratford-upon-Avon. He also inherited his father's house when his father died in 1601. In 1611, Shakespeare retired and moved back to Stratford-upon-Avon. He died on the 23rd April 1616, his 52nd birthday, and was buried at Holy Trinity Church in Stratford-upon-Avon.

Source of the Play

The source of *Macbeth* is found in 'The Chronicles of Scotland*', by Raphael Holinshed which was published around 1577. Shakespeare adapted the story for political reasons, mainly to flatter King James 1st, who was King of England at the time. In the original story both Macbeth and Banquo plotted to murder King Duncan. However, as King James was a descendant of Banquo, Shakespeare realised it would not be very pleasing for him to learn that his ancestor was a murderer, and therefore Banquo remains innocent in Shakespeare's version. King James would have been familiar with the story and of his ancestor's history. He would not have wanted to be associated with regicide* and therefore it was necessary for Shakespeare to change the real history into a work of fiction.

King James and his Influence on the Play

Shakespeare wrote *Macbeth* in 1606 and it was first performed to entertain James 1st of England (6th of Scotland), who became King after the childless Elizabeth 1st. Elizabeth died without an heir and it was her sister Mary's son who was to become King of England, even though at the time, he was already King of Scotland. *Macbeth* was first performed at Hampton Court where King James lived.

As well as including some of King James' ancestors, Shakespeare was aware of his wish to pass on his titles and lands to a male heir and the play reflected this in Duncan announcing that Malcolm (his eldest son), would become his heir. Naturally, this pleased James 1st as he would have recognised his own policy. The plot of *Macbeth* was also influenced by King James on another level. He was very interested in witch-hunting and the supernatural, and considered himself quite an expert. Witch-hunting was considered an activity for intelligent people, and King James believed strongly that witches existed. The witches profess the ability to predict the future, and the evil that could result from this knowledge is at the heart of the play. In the play, Shakespeare demonstrates to his audience how dangerous the supernatural could be. God ruled heaven and earth and the King ruled by God's appointment. Working with the supernatural was against all wishes of God and could only bring evil and tragedy. Shakespeare uses this message throughout the play to show both the power and the evil of the supernatural. King James would have acknowledged this and recognised Shakespeare's clever inclusion of his favourite subject.

The Divine Right of Kings

The Divine Right of Kings* was an idea that started in the Middle Ages. It was believed that God had appointed the King, and the King had absolute power. His authority was never challenged, and he ruled with the will of God. If someone was to remove the

King from power, it was going against the will of God and was a sin. It also went against the religious doctrine* taught at the time. Any attempt to kill the King was considered treason and punished by immediate death. Kings expected complete obedience from all of their subjects, including the thanes, their councillors and their own wives. Only God could judge the King and an unfair King was punished by God. In *Macbeth*, King Duncan is murdered by Macbeth; this was seen as the greatest crime anyone could commit and the audience would be left in no doubt of the seriousness of the crime and its consequences. The death of Macbeth at the end of the play is justified as the will of God for disobeying Him.

The Gunpowder Plot

The Gunpowder Plot was a plot to blow up the Houses of Parliament in London, where all the laws of the land were made. The plan was to blow up Parliament on the 5th November 1605, during the State Opening, which would be attended by King James. The plotters were all devoted Catholics and wished for England to become a Catholic country. One of the main plotters, Guy Fawkes, was responsible for the explosives to be used and it is his name that is remembered more than any of the others. We still celebrate the failure of the plot today on Bonfire Night. The plot was revealed when an anonymous letter, sent by one of the plotters, tried to warn a relative who was a Member of Parliament. At around midnight on the 4th November there was a search of the Houses of Parliament, and Guy Fawkes was found guarding 36 barrels of gunpowder, which was more than enough to blow up the whole House and everyone in it, including King James. Guy Fawkes was arrested and tortured along with some of the other plotters.

Although the Gunpowder Plot failed, it greatly affected King James and whilst previously he was tolerant of all religions, after the Gunpowder Plot, he and his government became anti-Catholic*. The Gunpowder Plot is significant to the play as it showed that a king has many enemies and he needed to be aware of what was happening at all times. He needed to trust his thanes, advisors and his army. In *Macbeth*, Macbeth begins to mistrust his thanes and decides to take matters into his own hands. His way of dealing with this mistrust is a series of calculated murders to rid him of anyone who might be a possible threat to him. Furthermore, just like Guy Fawkes, Macbeth is also killed for his killing of the King, which served as a harsh reminder to King James' opponents that they would be killed if they attempted to overthrow him.

Religion

The main religion in England during the time of Shakespeare was Protestantism*. Protestantism had been declared the national religion of England one year before Shakespeare's birth in 1564. Attending the Church of England was compulsory and people had to pay fines if they did not attend. People believed in God, heaven and hell, and they also believed that their behaviour on this earth would reflect where they went after death. The churches were often very wealthy and had the right to judge the people, and to take a percentage of their lands and goods. Shakespeare understood his audience very well. Writing a play where the characters are mostly good or mostly wicked provided a contrast that the audience could understand, but more importantly it taught a moral lesson to the audience about the danger of defying the laws of the Church of England, such as murder and treason. Shakespeare knew what effect the murder of King Duncan would have on his audience. Their immediate reaction would be that of horror and fear and they would expect some form of revenge for King Duncan.

The Role of Women

The primary role of women in the time of Shakespeare was to marry and have children. The death rate for young children was very high and women were expected to produce children roughly every two years. Women were not allowed to inherit any lands or titles from their fathers and because of this, marriages were often arranged for financial reasons rather than for love. This meant that wealthy women in particular were under pressure to produce a male heir who could inherit the title, money and land. Women with a title such as Lady Macbeth were expected to behave appropriately as fit their position. They must obey their husbands, fathers or brothers, be able to entertain guests and generally behave in a lady-like manner.

Lady Macbeth is not considered a traditional woman. She is ambitious and ruthless and is ready to defy her husband's authority and to ignore the position of King Duncan. The audience would be shocked by her behaviour in two ways:

- Calling on the spirit world to give her the powers she needs to become brave and fearless.
- Her disregard of her husband's wishes, and the intensity of her persuasion to get Macbeth to kill the King.

Lady Macbeth's behaviour served as a warning to the audience that women should never disobey their husbands, nor interfere in the spirit world.

Before the rule of King James, England was ruled by a woman, Queen Elizabeth 1st until her death in 1603. When she died, she remained a very popular ruler and many of her supporters were unhappy about James becoming King. Therefore, by creating a power-hungry, dangerous woman in Lady Macbeth, Shakespeare was showing the danger of women in power to his Jacobean audience. She was going against all the traditional roles of women, just as Queen Elizabeth did by becoming Queen and Shakespeare hoped that this display of evil would also please the male King.

The Purpose of the Play

The play is a tragedy, full of action and drama. Its purpose was primarily to entertain, but it carried moral messages and showed the difference between good and evil and the supernatural and the normal.

It was clever of Shakespeare to write a play which not only entertained James 1st but complimented him as a King who demonstrated good qualities. The King would expect an ending where the rightful King of Scotland triumphed over the evil and tyrannical usurper (someone who took a position of power illegally or by force, as in the case of Macbeth).

Shakespeare developed Macbeth into a complex figure with a strong conscience, who is tempted by the powers of the supernatural. Macbeth turns his back on his moral conscience and the play demonstrated how this would have devastating results.

Progress and Revision Check

1. What affected William Shakespeare's decision to become a playwright?
2. What three genres of play did Shakespeare write?
3. In what book did Shakespeare read the original story of *Macbeth*?
4. What are some of the reasons that Shakespeare adapted the original story?
5. What was the normal role of women in the time of Shakespeare?
6. What main event happened in 1605 which affected King James 1st?
7. What was the main religion in England during Shakespeare's time?
8. Why was religion important in the time of Shakespeare?
9. Explain what is meant by the phrase 'The Divine Right of Kings'.
10. Why did Shakespeare create Lady Macbeth as a dangerous woman?

~ THE PLAY – SUMMARY AND ANALYSIS ~

Who's Who

Main Characters

Macbeth – the tragic hero* who falls from a position of power after meeting the witches and murdering Duncan. Macbeth was Thane (lord) of Glamis and was also given the title of Thane of Cawdor. He is a brave and faithful commander in Duncan's army and by his own hand becomes the King of Scotland. Unfortunately for Macbeth, the murder of King Duncan seals his downfall and he is eventually killed.

Lady Macbeth – Macbeth's wife and partner in the murder of Duncan. Lady Macbeth is portrayed as ruthless and ambitious, but she is loved and trusted by Macbeth. Their loving relationship deteriorates as the play progresses and Lady Macbeth takes her own life at the end of the play.

Banquo – a commander in the army and good friend of Macbeth, who is well respected by his fellow officers and the King. Although he is present when Macbeth meets the witches, he is not tempted by them and remains rational and sceptical of their predictions. He is murdered by Macbeth.

Duncan – King of Scotland. He is a kind and fair king and reinforces the Jacobean belief that he was appointed by God and is almost a divine presence on earth.

The Three Witches – supernatural beings sometimes called "the weird sisters". They deliver prophecies to Macbeth and Banquo throughout the play and claim to predict the future.

Macduff – a thane who is a faithful and loyal servant to King Duncan. Macduff closely watches Macbeth and is suspicious of him. Alongside Malcolm, he leads the opposition to Macbeth and finally kills him.

Minor Characters

Malcolm and Donaldbain – Duncan's two sons. The eldest, Malcolm, is next in line to the throne after the death of Duncan and is seen as a prime suspect in the murder of his father. Both sons flee from Scotland after the murder of their father. Malcolm eventually raises an army in England, with the help of Macduff, and is crowned king after the death of Macbeth.

Fleance – the son of Banquo. Macbeth plots to have his murderers kill Fleance but he escapes.

Lady Macduff – Macduff's wife who, along with her son, is brutally murdered by Macbeth's evil henchmen.

Siward – Earl of Northumberland.

Young Siward – Siward's son who fights Macbeth but is killed by Macbeth's sword.

Seyton – Macbeth's servant.

The Porter – gate keeper at Macbeth's castle.

The following characters are all Thanes of Scotland and help to rule the kingdom:

Lennox
Ross
Menteith
Angus
Caithness

The Play

Act 1

Act 1 Scene 1 – The introduction of the witches

The start of the play is a very short scene and portrays three witches deciding on when and where they will meet, and who they are meeting. The witches are not human; they look frightening and ugly. The scene appears menacing as it is set on the battlefield with thunder and lightning which add to the drama. The turbulent weather suggests chaos, and the evil-looking witches demonstrate a frightening presence to the audience.

Analysis

The witches speak in rhyming couplets which differs from the blank verse used by the rest of the characters. The significance of this is that it sounds like chanting and this makes the audience aware that they are a supernatural force. The audience enter the scene at the end of the meeting between the witches. This is significant as we do not know what has gone before but are aware that these supernatural beings are plotting something. The purpose of this first scene is to set the mood of the play. The sight of the witches and chaotic weather conditions add to the tension and foreshadow the chaos that Scotland will be thrown into by Macbeth.

Act 1 Scene 2 – Duncan rewards Macbeth

Macbeth and his good friend and brave soldier Banquo are returning from the battlefield, where they have successfully beaten their enemies. In King Duncan's headquarters, the King is informed of the battle and the selfless bravery of Macbeth. He decides that the title 'Thane of Cawdor' will be given to Macbeth as a reward for his bravery in battle and his defeat of the enemy. Duncan is told by Ross that the first Thane of Cawdor had become: "A most disloyal traitor" and Duncan immediately pronounces his death.

Analysis

The scene establishes King Duncan's character, as well as the reputation of Macbeth. Duncan shows how he can be a generous king and also someone who will act promptly when necessary. His swift dealing of the traitor demonstrates this. Macbeth does not appear in the scene but the Captain describes him as: "brave Macbeth – well he deserves that name—". This is significant as his reputation is established before he enters the play and the audience is introduced to a morally good man and a fearless soldier. However, there is irony* in the scene as Duncan will find out to his cost that Macbeth too is a "A most disloyal traitor". Shakespeare purposefully foreshadows Macbeth's disloyalty through the death of the Thane of Cawdor.

Act 1 Scene 3 – Macbeth and Banquo meet the witches

The three weird witches enter again and they meet the battle-weary Macbeth and Banquo. The first witch greets Macbeth with: "All hail Macbeth, hail to thee, Thane of Glamis", followed by the second witch: "All hail Macbeth, hail to thee, Thane of Cawdor". The third witch greets Macbeth with: "All hail Macbeth, that shalt be King hereafter". Macbeth is stunned by what they say. They greet Banquo in a similar way to Macbeth, but significantly, do not suggest that he will be King himself. The first witch describes him as "Lesser than Macbeth and greater", while the second witch follows with: "Not so happy yet much happier". Finally, the third witch predicts: "thou shalt get kings though thou be none". Almost immediately after the witches vanish, two of Duncan's messengers bring news of a new honour to Macbeth, the Thane of Cawdor. With this message, the second prophecy of the witches has suddenly come true. This makes Macbeth think that becoming King is a very real possibility.

Analysis

The three witches, speaking separately, gives them all equal importance, as well as making them appear more menacing, especially as the audience is aware that it is Macbeth's bravery and not the witches' magic that has earned him his new title. Shakespeare purposely creates a contrast between Banquo and Macbeth here, as Banquo hears the witches' predictions but is more disbelieving and wonders if he and Macbeth have been tricked by madness. Macbeth has other thoughts however and is much more inclined to believe the witches. He becomes preoccupied and begins to speak his thoughts out loud in his soliloquy. He begins to fantasise about becoming King and the thoughts frighten him. The scene is significant as it introduces the themes of ambition and fate. Through this contrast, Shakespeare introduces to the audience that Banquo is a foil for Macbeth; he represents to the audience what would happen if Macbeth had chosen not to listen to the witches.

Act 1 Scene 4 – Duncan announces the next King

Duncan is in his headquarters and decides to ensure his son Malcolm will become the next King, by declaring "We will establish our estate upon our eldest, Malcolm, whom we name hereafter, The Prince of Cumberland". This is significant as, on returning to the headquarters of the King, Macbeth learns of Duncan's decision, and realises that it will be impossible for him to claim the throne unless something is done. Macbeth is frightened by his own thoughts of murdering the King, but his ambition and desire to fulfil the witches' prophecies remain.

Analysis

Macbeth now has the motive to kill the King. Shakespeare shows how Macbeth's character is beginning to change; his attitude appears to have hardened and he is more determined to commit murder and treachery, recognising that his mind is filled with "black and deep desires", with the colour black representing the corruption of his hidden thoughts. The scene is significant as it helps to establish a reason for Macbeth to murder King Duncan and appears to be the beginning of Macbeth's downfall.

Act 1 Scene 5 – Macbeth informs Lady Macbeth of the prophecies

Macbeth sends a letter to his wife to inform her of the witches' predictions and to tell her that the King and his men will be arriving at their castle later that day as their guests. Lady Macbeth is delighted by the news of his letter. She immediately begins to plot the murder of the King but is worried because she knows Macbeth's personal weakness of being filled with "the milk of human kindness", suggesting he is emotionally too weak to fulfil her wishes. She sets out to persuade Macbeth that the King must be murdered that night to secure their future as rulers of Scotland. Lady Macbeth calls upon supernatural powers to help her become greater than a woman and have the strength of will to persuade her husband to murder the King: "Come, you spirits that tend on mortal thoughts, unsex me here, and fill me from the crown to the toe topfull of direst cruelty".

Analysis

This scene is important in establishing the relationship that Macbeth has with his wife. Because the letter can be interpreted as treason, the fact that he tells her the prophecies shows how much he feels he can trust her. By calling on supernatural forces, Lady Macbeth emphasises how truly wicked she is. Furthermore, by using imperative verbs such as "come" and "unsex" to appeal to the spirit world, Lady Macbeth has already changed from her gentle personality to someone far more dangerous, as it seems she is now commanding the supernatural. It is a clever method by Shakespeare of demonstrating her growing power. A Jacobean audience would be shocked by the behaviour of Lady Macbeth, not only because of her wicked thoughts, but also of her intentions to control her husband, which would have been seen as inappropriate for a woman.

Act 1 Scene 6 – Duncan comes to Macbeth's castle

Duncan arrives at the castle of Macbeth and is greeted by Lady Macbeth. The King showers compliments on Lady Macbeth and they walk into the castle together. The King is eager to meet Macbeth and to thank him for his brave conduct in battle; however, Macbeth does not come to the door to greet the King.

Analysis

This scene is important because it shows how reality can differ from appearance. Lady Macbeth is plotting to have the King murdered but she goes along with the pretence that she is delighted to have the King as her guest and behaves with great courtesy. This demonstrates her cunning and just how dangerous she can be. The King has no idea that she is being dishonest which shows his faith and trust in his people. Furthermore, it is significant that Macbeth does not greet the King and suggests that

Lady Macbeth has already begun to take control of the situation. She is the face of the castle and of the plot to kill the King.

Act 1 Scene 7 – Macbeth has doubts

The scene shows Macbeth at his most vulnerable. Whilst he is alone, he speaks aloud his inner thoughts in a soliloquy and wrestles with his own conscience. He knows that Duncan is a great king and to murder him would mean damnation. Macbeth realises that he should be protecting the King, not contemplating murdering him. He feels that it is only "vaulting ambition" that is driving him on, and he will "proceed no further". Lady Macbeth decides to intervene; she cannot let the opportunity to murder King Duncan slip away from them. She urges Macbeth to murder Duncan while he sleeps, explaining that he will use the daggers of the King's guards to kill Duncan and after the deed is done, will smear the guards in the blood of Duncan, which will automatically lead to their guilt. The guards will be drugged to ensure they sleep through the murder. The plan appears flawless and Macbeth finally agrees to the murder.

Analysis

This scene is significant to the play as it is Lady Macbeth who, having anticipated that there is a weakness in Macbeth's character, seizes her opportunity to persuade him. Her strategy is to insult Macbeth regarding his manliness and his cowardice. She is raging with anger at his decision and accuses him of breaking a promise. Here, Shakespeare further explores the relationship between Macbeth and his wife and demonstrates the strength of her persuasion and power. Lady Macbeth shows how strong her ambition is, which juxtaposes with Macbeth's weakness. Shakespeare contrasts her behaviour to that of the normal role of women in her position to unsettle the audience and to heighten concerns about their relationship. No good can come from a relationship where the woman is so dominant.

Act 2

Act 2 Scene 1 – Macbeth is haunted by what he is about to do

Banquo and his son are preparing for bed. The tension of the night and what has happened during the day is felt by Banquo and this becomes apparent when he speaks to his son Fleance: "there's husbandry in heaven, their candles are all out", suggesting that the dark night has no light whatsoever. They encounter Macbeth and they discuss the meeting of the witches, but Macbeth tells Banquo that he thinks "not of them". Macbeth is not being honest to his friend and this is a trait which continues throughout the play. After leaving Banquo, Macbeth dismisses his servant and begins to consider the task ahead of him. Macbeth prepares himself to commit murder.

Analysis

Once again, the supernatural intervenes and this intervention repeats itself throughout the play. Alone, he begins to hallucinate in one of the most famous of Shakespeare's soliloquys: "Is this a dagger I see before me the handle toward my hand?" Macbeth uses a rhetorical question to open his speech, which not only demonstrates his confusion at the situation he finds himself in, but also that he is willing to accept the intervention of the supernatural as it is pointing towards his hand, as if it was ready for him to take and carry out the murder. In this soliloquy, his rational mind is fully overtaken by his ambition and the audience witness his fall from the "brave" character in Act 1.

Act 2 Scene 2 – Macbeth murders the King

Lady Macbeth is very tense while she is waiting for her husband to finish the deadly deed. He returns to his wife after murdering Duncan, but he is afraid and brings the bloody daggers back with him. While Lady Macbeth awaits her husband's return, she has been drinking some wine to give herself the courage she needs. She sees that Macbeth has returned with the bloody daggers and takes control of the situation by telling him to go back and smear the blood on the guards and leave the daggers with them. Macbeth can no longer move such is his guilt and fear. Lady Macbeth takes the daggers back to the guards, which shows the audience that her resolve is stronger than his. They retire to their bedroom but shortly hear a loud knocking at the south door of the castle.

Analysis

This scene is important as now the deed is done, there is no turning back. The murder of Duncan is not shown to the audience, as in Shakespeare's time something as horrific as regicide would have been too terrible to watch, even in a play, but the horror of what Macbeth has done is shown by his speech when he cannot return the daggers: "I'll go no more. I am afraid to think what I have done; Look on't again, I dare not". Even Macbeth cannot bring himself to return to the scene of the crime, such is the seriousness of what he has done. This scene is also significant as it shows how Lady Macbeth's character develops into someone stronger than her husband. She will not let the plan fail. She takes the daggers back to the guards, smearing them with the blood of Duncan and incriminating them in the murder. However, by taking the daggers from Macbeth, Lady Macbeth is literally and metaphorically* putting the blood on her hands. The blood on her hands represents the part that she also plays in the murder and this is why she must also suffer at the end of the play.

Act 2 Scene 3 – Macduff finds the dead King

Scene 3 begins with some light relief as the old porter wakes from a drunken sleep after the constant knocking on the door of the castle. This is an important scene as it helps to relieve the tension of the previous scene by adding humour in the form of inappropriate comments regarding drink and sex. His speech is vulgar and humorous and serves to alleviate the tension of the horrific scene that has gone before. Macduff and Lennox are at the door of the castle. They have come on request by the King to wake him early. Tension builds in the audience, as we know what Macduff will find in the King's chamber. Macduff goes to the King's chamber to find him murdered. He screams for the guests to wake and the bell to be rung: "Ring the alarum bell! Murder and Treason!" Macbeth, in his wild passion (and perhaps because of his guilt) kills the guards who are sleeping peacefully but covered in blood. Lady Macbeth faints or pretends to faint at the sight of the blood, possibly to take the attention away from Macbeth's murdering of the guards. Donaldbain and Malcolm, the sons of Duncan, observe what has happened and, realising they are in danger, decide to leave immediately, compromising their own innocence by their flight.

Analysis

Although the porter's references and jokes are not very funny to a modern audience, a Jacobean audience would understand the humour. The porter's quote comparing Macbeth's castle to hell is ironic. The porter describes the Castle as being "Too cold for Hell". The fact that the castle is too cold for a place that is symbolised* by burning heat and fire suggests that there is no emotion or warmth in the castle, which would be chilling for the audience. The porter refers to his job of gatekeeper as being like the gatekeeper of hell: "I'll devil-porter it no further". This is significant as although the porter doesn't know it, Duncan has just been murdered and therefore the castle of Macbeth has become a kind of hell.

The significance of this scene is:

- to bring some light relief to the tension of the murder, through the porter's speech
- to heighten the tension even further at the discovery of Duncan's body
- to allow Macbeth to seize the opportunity to become King of Scotland through the flight of Duncan's sons

Act 2 Scene 4 – Macduff is suspicious of Macbeth

This is a short scene with Ross and an old man recalling the night of the murder. Ross feels the night was very strange; Duncan's horses "turn'd wild in nature" suggesting a supernatural influence. Macduff enters the scene and tells them that Duncan's two sons have fled and that Macbeth will become King and be crowned at Scone.

Analysis

The purpose of this scene is to show a passing of time and to suggest that there is evil around as horses, known for their instincts, behaved wildly at the time of Duncan's murder. It is also an important scene as Macduff becomes more prominent as a character. He has decided to defy Macbeth and not attend Macbeth's coronation. This defiance suggests that Macduff may be suspicious of Macbeth and foreshadows his role in Macbeth's downfall.

Act 3

Act 3 Scene 1 – Banquo is suspicious of Macbeth

Banquo thinks about the witches' prophecies; he feels that something is not right. He does not trust Macbeth and is suspicious of him. The audience sees Banquo question Macbeth's loyalty when he says: "Thou hast it now, king, Cawdor, Glamis, all, As the weird woman promis'd, and I fear thou played'st most foully for't". After this, Macbeth speaks a soliloquy which tells the audience of his fear of Banquo. He contemplates the prophecies of the witches and realises that he cannot be safe as long as Banquo and Fleance are alive.

Analysis

This scene further emphasises the contrast between Banquo and Macbeth. Banquo has heard the prediction from the witches but has not reacted in the same way as Macbeth; he does not take any action to make the predictions come true. Banquo explains that although Macbeth has proven the witches' predictions correct, he believes that Macbeth has achieved them by evil means. Shakespeare demonstrates that Banquo is honourable and should be trusted, but Macbeth shows weakness and fear. Macbeth's behaviour here is similar to his wife's when she greets King Duncan. He pretends that all is well and is polite to Banquo, knowing that he needs to rid himself of both Banquo and Fleance to keep his position safe.

Act 3 Scene 2 – Macbeth is fearful of Banquo

After Macbeth's coronation, a grand banquet is arranged and Macbeth wants Banquo, his loyal friend, to be the chief guest. He tries to act naturally towards Banquo, but he has already plotted to have him and his son murdered. Macbeth fears the prophecies that the witches predicted for Banquo will come true and realises that his crown is unsafe. Macbeth knows that if the witches' predictions are true for him, they must also be true for Banquo and Fleance: "there is none but he, whose being I do fear". He must rid himself of all who may be a danger to him. Confirming that Banquo and his son will be out riding, he has planned for two of his henchmen to kill them. It is both cruel and cowardly as he asks the murderers: "to leave no rubs nor botches in the work".

Analysis

This is a significant scene as Banquo is Macbeth's trusted friend and a brave soldier. To have him and his son Fleance murdered in cold blood shows how suspicious Macbeth has become and he clearly trusts no one, not even his best friend. It is also important as it exposes the kind of rule Macbeth will undertake – he will be a tyrant who will not work with other thanes but instead will act selfishly and for his own benefit. Macbeth keeps his plans from his wife, suggesting that their relationship is weakening, which is in stark contrast to Act 1 Scene 5 where Macbeth tells his wife of his actions.

Shakespeare cleverly influences the audience by allowing them to become aware of the differences between Macbeth and Banquo through Macbeth's cruel scheme to have Banquo and his son murdered. Any sympathies the audience might have for Macbeth are gone in this scene.

Act 3 Scene 3 – Banquo is murdered but Fleance escapes

The murderers lie in wait for Banquo and Fleance. Banquo is killed but manages to call out to his son: "O, treachery! Fly, good Fleance fly, fly, fly! Thou may'st revenge— O slave!" Fleance escapes and the murderers know that they have only managed half of the contract they were asked to complete.

Analysis

It is interesting to note that there are three murderers in this scene. Macbeth does not trust that the job will be done and therefore has the men work in threes to further highlight his lack of trust in anyone, even the evil thugs sent to do his dirty work. However, despite the efforts of Macbeth to have Banquo and Fleance murdered, the witches have the upper hand, as Fleance escapes to fulfil their prophecies. It also demonstrates how Macbeth has become ruthless in his striving for power.

Act 3 Scene 4 – Macbeth sees the ghost of Banquo

At a banquet in honour of Banquo, Macbeth appears to be the generous host, drinking and sharing a cup of wine with his guests. The ghost of Banquo, bloody and injured, enters the banquet, but can only be seen by Macbeth. Macbeth is terrified and starts to behave irrationally, while his wife makes excuses for her husband's behaviour by saying: "My lord is often thus, and hath been from his youth. Pray you keep seat". The ghost disappears, and Macbeth is able to go back to his guests and behave more reasonably once more, until Banquo's ghost reappears, Macbeth is unable to keep his composure and breaks down, almost revealing his guilt. Lady Macbeth, seeing his distress, realises there is nothing to be done and dismisses the guests.

Analysis

The banquet opens with Macbeth sharing a cup of wine with his guests. This is supposed to be a symbolic gesture that demonstrates unity and friendship to his fellow thanes, but the audience is aware that this is a pretence by Macbeth to hide his truly evil nature. This scene marks the beginning of the deterioration in Macbeth's power and the rule he has over the thanes. His behaviour is distressing in the presence of his most important guests and demonstrates how Lady Macbeth tries to suppress his behaviour with her explanations, but the guests have seen enough to be cautious of Macbeth. He is not behaving in a kingly manner and his power is diminishing. Shakespeare uses the scene to continue the theme of the supernatural by using the image of Banquo's bloodied ghost as a sign of the powers of the supernatural. No matter how he tries to protect his power, the image of Banquo's ghost represents the guilt that Macbeth feels for the evil actions that he has carried out.

Act 3 Scene 5 – The witches prepare a spell to trick Macbeth

The witches and Hecate, who is their queen, prepare to meet Macbeth once again. Hecate is angry with them for offering prophecies to Macbeth without telling her and she decides to make a very powerful and intoxicating spell to trick Macbeth.

Analysis

The forces of the supernatural are apparent in this short scene. The scene reminds the audience again of the supernatural elements in the play and its link with Macbeth. The powers of the supernatural have changed Macbeth, and Hecate refers to him as a "wayward son", suggesting he, like them, is full of evil. Shakespeare's purpose is to upset the audience with this short scene. By describing him as their "son", Macbeth may become like the supernatural spirits with no fear and no conscience. The audience fear the outcome for Macbeth.

Act 3 Scene 6 – Macbeth loses the respect of the thanes

Time progresses and the tyrannous rule of Macbeth continues. Suspicion of Macbeth grows. Lennox speaks about Macbeth, but he is not speaking on his own behalf, but rather on behalf of the Scottish people. He speaks of the distrust of the people over Macbeth's traitorous behaviour. The audience learns that Macduff has decided to join Malcolm in England.

Analysis

This scene is significant as it shows that Macbeth, through his behaviour at the banquet and his harsh rule, has lost the respect of the thanes as well as the common people. Lennox is sarcastic in his tone when he speaks of Macbeth's behaviour at the death of Duncan: "How it did grieve Macbeth!" suggesting that the thanes now suspect Macbeth's part in Duncan's murder and the mask that he wore at the beginning of the banquet scene is slipping. Furthermore, the audience will recognise the significance of Macduff going to England to find Malcolm; this further indicates his distrust of Macbeth.

Act 4

Act 4 Scene 1 – Macbeth receives more prophecies

Macbeth decides to seek further advice from the witches to find out what his future may now hold. The three witches meet on a wild heath again to greet Macbeth and declare his destiny. Macbeth demands they answer his questions and three apparitions show themselves to Macbeth. The witches are brewing up a spell to trick him. They add repulsive items to the mix repeating the phrase: "Double, double toil and trouble, fire burn and cauldron bubble". Finally, the second witch completes the spell with the words: "Cool it with a baboon's blood, then the charm is firm and good".

With the spell ready, the witches await the return of Macbeth who asks them to tell him more about the future. He is told three prophecies:

- a floating head warns him he should "beware Macduff"
- a child covered in blood tells him that no man born of woman can harm him
- a child wearing a crown and holding a tree declares Macbeth cannot be defeated until Birnam Wood marches to Dunsinane Hill

Finally, he is shown a strange vision of eight kings in a line, with Banquo's ghost at the end of the line, the final king holding a mirror. Macbeth does not understand these apparitions and is only concerned with the prophecies that tell him of the warnings and the fact that he cannot be harmed by man. Lennox arrives at the end of the scene and tells Macbeth that Macduff has fled to England and this leads Macbeth to make the decision that he will kill Macduff's wife and children.

Analysis

The purpose of this scene is to show how Macbeth has turned into a wicked, sinful and unnatural human being. The spell of the witches is made up of some terrible things; a baboon was seen as an evil and jealous creature and its blood used in the spell would be understood by the audience as toxic. The fact that this spell is for Macbeth emphasises how even the supernatural witches believe him to be evil also. Shakespeare's symbolism in the apparitions is evident and appear to outline the future of Scotland. The line of kings is a reference to Banquo's sons and descendants, who will rule over Scotland and represent the fact that Macbeth will fail in his quest to maintain the crown of Scotland. Furthermore, the fact that the final king holds a mirror is a clever ploy by Shakespeare as King James will have seen his reflection in that mirror, which represents his rightful place as the King of England. Despite the clear warnings by the witches, Macbeth feels invincible as he turns towards evil once again and, without remorse, decides to murder the wife and children of Macduff.

Act 4 Scene 2 – Lady Macduff and her son are murdered

Lady Macduff has been told by Ross that her husband has fled to England, but she is loyal and doesn't think her husband would become a traitor. Soon after, a messenger arrives urging her to leave as she is in danger. However, the murderers arrive too soon and both she and her son are murdered.

Analysis

This scene is somewhat sad, as Lady Macduff and her son are horrifically killed. Macbeth has no reason to be fearful of Lady Macduff but still goes ahead with the murders. The fact that Macbeth is now killing innocent women and children would have reinforced Macbeth's violence to the audience and they would have been shocked at his brutality. This scene and the horrific events that take place, further highlight that Macbeth's character cannot be redeemed.

Act 4 Scene 3 – Macduff plots with Malcolm

Macduff arrives in England to try and persuade Malcolm to lead the English army to fight and overcome Macbeth and claim what is rightfully his. Malcolm does not trust Macduff; he does not fully understand why he has left his family. Macduff must prove he is loyal to Malcolm. Malcolm refers to Scotland as sick and injured: "I think our country sinks beneath the yoke: it weeps, it bleeds, and each new day a gash is added to her wounds". He refers to Macbeth as: "This tyrant, whose sole name blisters our tongue, was once thought honest". Ross has come to tell Macduff of the terrible news that his wife and son have been murdered. Macduff is overcome by grief but is urged by Malcolm to: "dispute it like a man", in other words to fight Macbeth. Driven by hatred and revenge, he vows to kill Macbeth.

Analysis

This scene effectively demonstrates to the audience that Malcolm has what it takes to be the rightful ruler of Scotland. He recognises that ruling selfishly like Macbeth makes Scotland "bleed". Furthermore, Macbeth is no longer referred to by his name, but is called a "tyrant", which represents that he is no longer recognisable as the man he once was. Shakespeare shows the humanity in Macduff by his grief on hearing about the murder of his wife and son. He responds to Malcolm by saying that he must "feel it as a man". Being a noble and good man is not just about being aggressive, but also about being in touch with one's emotions. The scene creates anticipation in the audience by suggesting Macduff is ready to avenge the deaths of his family as well as highlighting Macbeth as the oppressor he has become.

Act 5

Act 5 Scene 1 – Lady Macbeth becomes ill

The scene begins with a doctor and a gentlewoman discussing the health of Lady Macbeth. Despite Lady Macbeth's resolve and ambition earlier in the play, the behaviour of her now tyrannical husband and the murders he has committed has made her ill. Lady Macbeth has become a shadow of her former self, characterised by the fact that she now sleepwalks. She cries out and frets about the blood she thinks she still sees on her hands.

Analysis

This is the final scene where the audience sees Lady Macbeth alive. Her dramatic downfall from the strong, powerful woman to someone mentally unstable is clear. In Act 2, she was determined that she would feel no ill effects from the murder of Duncan, but she now sleepwalks and constantly goes over the night of the murder and her hands are metaphorically* stained with the blood of Duncan forever. After the killing of Duncan, she was happy to believe that she could wash the blood from her hands with "A little water". Yet in this scene, she says: "here's the smell of blood still; all the perfumes of Arabia will not sweeten this little hand". Lady Macbeth realises the enormity of what she and Macbeth have done and it seems that this has driven her to madness. Shakespeare's purpose here is to show how dangerous it is for women to have power and what fate has in store for powerful women. Lady Macbeth has challenged the traditional role of the noble woman in the time of Shakespeare. She had defied God by calling on the supernatural and asking them to take away her human emotions. The audience is in no doubt as to the consequences of rejecting God, and would have been expecting her downfall because of this.

Act 5 Scene 2 – The army from England arrives at Birnam Wood

Macduff, Malcolm and the English army have arrived in Scotland and are coming towards Birnam Wood. The thanes meet with Macduff and Malcolm. Angus says of Macbeth: "Now does he feel his secret murders sticking on his hands". It is clear that all the thanes are now aware of Macbeth's evil actions. They discuss that Macbeth is preparing for war at his castle.

Analysis

This scene is important as it builds the tension for the following scenes in anticipation of the climax of the play. Angus's quote suggests that the blood of Macbeth's enemies stays on his hands forever and that he realises the consequence of his actions.

Act 5 Scene 3 – Macbeth hears about his wife's illness

Macbeth continues to tell those in his castle that he cannot be harmed and has nothing to fear from Malcolm's army because of the witches' prophecies, even after his servant, Seyton, tells him that there is an army of ten thousand men marching towards him. Macbeth hears of his wife's ill health from her doctor. Macbeth queries whether the doctor can cure his wife. He also asks the doctor for his opinion on the health of the country. This is asked with grim humour and the doctor closes the scene with a telling warning: "Were I from Dunsinane away and clear. Profit again should hardly draw me here".

Analysis

Once again, Shakespeare portrays Macbeth as delusional; he does not seem to understand that he cannot escape his downfall because of his misunderstanding of the prophecies. Furthermore, the fact that his servant is called Seyton (pronounced Satan) is another clever inclusion by Shakespeare to highlight how evil Macbeth has become; it seems as if even the devil serves him. Ironically Macbeth would like the doctor to 'cure' the country: "If thou couldst doctor, cast / The water of my land, find her disease, / And purge it to a sound and pristine health". This quote suggests that Macbeth knows that the country is troubled and that his thanes have left him, but he has no understanding to the reason why. It is significant that even the doctor feels the need to leave. Doctors were known for their greed and need for profit in treating patients, but even money cannot persuade him to stay and he will not return.

Act 5 Scene 4 – Macbeth and Macduff prepare for battle

Macduff has issued orders that his soldiers camouflage themselves with the branches from Birnam Wood. Macbeth fortifies his castle whilst his courtiers prepare to leave, fearing Macbeth is mad. Macbeth hears that Birnam Wood is moving and marching towards his castle. The witches warned him about this, but he believes it cannot possibly happen. Macbeth does not realise that the English army is camouflaged, and he prepares himself for battle.

Analysis

This scene reminds the audience of the significance of the witches' prophecies. It is important to understand Macbeth's character at this point. He has full trust in the witches and believes no harm can come to him. The audience is fully aware of what is about to happen. This dramatic irony* makes his downfall even more satisfying as he does not see it coming.

Act 5 Scene 5 – Macbeth is told of his wife's death

Macbeth boasts of his confidence and victory in battle. When he hears a woman scream, his servant goes to investigate, and he is told of his wife's death. He barely reacts and simply comments: "She should have died hereafter". Instead, he dwells on the pointlessness of life and talks about the "petty pace from day to day". A messenger enters and tells him that Birnam Wood is approaching.

Analysis

Shakespeare leaves the audience wondering about Macbeth's quote regarding his wife's death. The word "hereafter" may refer to the future in this comment, but it is clear that Macbeth is so preoccupied by his own troubles that he speaks of the death of his once loving and loyal wife without emotion and continues with a very depressing speech which shows the hopelessness of his situation. It is clear that he has abandoned everything that he once loved because of his ambition.

Act 5 Scenes 6–10 – Macbeth is killed by Macduff

Macduff calls for the battle sound to be made as the army nears the castle. Macbeth warns young Siward that no man born of woman can harm him. Even still, young Siward bravely fights Macbeth but is killed in the process.

Macbeth claims:

> "Thou wast born of woman.
> But swords I smile at, weapons laugh to scorn,
> Brandish'd by man that's of woman born."

Macbeth, still believing he is invincible, awaits his enemies. He meets Macduff and repeats his prophecy, but Macduff tells him that:

> "Despair thy charm,
> And let the angel whom thou still hast serv'd
> Tell thee, Macduff was from his mother's womb
> Untimely ripp'd."

Macduff and Macbeth fight and Macbeth is killed by Macduff.

Analysis

These scenes are very short but full of action, which is in contrast to the longer scenes of previous acts. Shakespeare has held the dramatic tension and Macbeth now, too late, realises the witches deceit, that "these juggling fiends" have tricked him, and he is killed. The juggling fiends refer to the three witches and the supernatural spells they made to convince Macbeth he was invincible. In his final moments, he has realised the dangers of the supernatural, but it is too late and he is punished for his error of listening to them. He has been tempted by the witches and has destroyed his conscience and honour in the process. Yet, despite the hopeless situation he finds himself in, the audience sees a glimpse of Macbeth the warrior once more when he tells Macduff: "Yet I will try the last". We see Macbeth as a fallen man but there are still some traces of his bravery and honour returning, but it is too late.

Act 5 Scene 11 – The rightful King returns

Macduff beheads the dead King. Victory is proclaimed and Malcolm announces that order will return to Scotland and the true king will be crowned at Scone. Malcolm refers to Macbeth and Lady Macbeth as: "this dead butcher and his fiend-like queen".

Analysis

The final quote by Malcolm about Macbeth and Lady Macbeth reminds us of the reign of terror that Macbeth has bestowed on Scotland and its people. The final scenes demonstrate just how evil supernatural powers are, and how the witches have deceived and misled Macbeth. He is left isolated, a man of pity, he has paid the price of his unyielding ambition. Malcolm and Macduff have found revenge and justice at the end of the play. Macduff has avenged his wife and son, and Malcolm has avenged his father. It is significant that Macbeth has been beheaded, just like the enemy in Act 1 Scene 2 who was beheaded by Macbeth. Justice has finally been served on Macbeth and it is a fitting climax of the play.

Progress and Revision Check

1. How do Macbeth and Banquo differ in their response to the witches?
2. How does Lady Macbeth react to the news from her husband about the witches' prophecies?
3. How does Macbeth feel about murdering Duncan in Act 1 Scene 7 and what are his reasons?
4. What does Macduff discover in Act 2 Scene 3 and what is his reaction?
5. What are the actions that Macbeth carries out immediately after the murder of Duncan?
6. How is Banquo killed?
7. Which character is Macbeth told to beware of by the witches?
8. What are the apparitions the witches conjure up in Act 4 Scene 1?
9. When does Macbeth realise that he has been deceived by magic?
10. Why would a Jacobean audience be satisfied with the ending of the play?

~ CHARACTERS ~

Macbeth

Macbeth the warrior

At the beginning of the play, Macbeth is described as a noble, brave and loyal warrior. After the battle, his reputation is well known in Scotland, and he is described to King Duncan as a man of great courage. At this stage there is no reason to consider Macbeth as anything but honourable and moral. He demonstrates an understanding of right and wrong, as well as loyalty to his king. He is well-liked and respected by the other thanes: "For brave Macbeth–well he deserves that name– /Disdaining Fortune, with his brandish'd steel, /which smoked with bloody execution" [Act 1 Scene 2].

Macbeth has proven himself by his violent actions. However, this violence may also be seen as a warning of the violence to come.

Macbeth's relationship with the witches

From the beginning, Macbeth puts his trust in the witches. He does not consider their words as evil or nonsense and this is reinforced by the information from Ross that he is the new Thane of Cawdor. However, his meeting with the witches reveals a darker side to his character. The witches' predictions have disturbed him deeply and their greetings have an overwhelming effect on him; the change in his personality is already beginning to show through in Act 1 Scene 4 when he describes his "black and deep desires", which highlight him as a man brooding on evil. It is important to pinpoint the changes in Macbeth and this quote can be used as a starting point to identify the beginning of his downfall. As the play progresses, Macbeth's trust in the witches becomes absolute. His ambition starts to unfold as he begins to think the predictions might come true. He does not appear to be frightened by the witches, and later Hecate, the queen of the witches, refers to him as a 'son', because he embraces their evil. Macbeth seeks out the witches when he needs to find out what the future will hold when he becomes King. This belief in the witches becomes a reliance and it is only at the end of the play that he realises the witches have tricked him and he was foolish to put his trust in them in the first place.

Macbeth's relationship with his wife

Macbeth has a very strong relationship with his wife; he loves her and calls her his "Dearest partner of greatness" [Act 1 Scene 5]. Shakespeare has used this quote to inform the audience of how much trust Macbeth places in his wife. She is not only his wife, but his "partner", which suggests that there is equality in their relationship, something which would have been unsettling for a Jacobean audience. The closeness of the couple is further revealed by the fact that Macbeth sends Lady Macbeth a letter informing her of the prophecies. Her influence could easily be dismissed if the partnership between them wasn't so strong. It may explain why Macbeth goes ahead with the murder of King Duncan.

Macbeth's ambition

Macbeth considers the prophecies but after thinking about the King's kindness and generosity he decides to go no further with the murderous action, declaring "we will proceed no further in this business" [Act 1 Scene 7]. He is a man who has wrestled with his conscience and decides to give up on his ambition to become King. This moral reasoning is a credit to Macbeth's character, but the strength of Lady Macbeth's persuasion and the flaws in his own personality such as pride, greed and desire, outweigh his honour and his resolve. After the murder of King Duncan, Macbeth begins to change or perhaps this dark, ambitious side of his character has always been part of the man. He is filled with ambition and realises that murdering the King would not be an end in itself and that this murder may be the first of many. The killing of Duncan has made him change and he allows ambition and greed to rule his life. He pursues further brutality with increasing ease of mind. At the beginning of the play he knew his role and his status in life – he was a loyal general and the Thane of Glamis, both honourable roles. However, the meeting of the witches, their foretelling of the future and this cold-blooded murder of the King has brought about an ambition stronger than his morality and conscience, and Macbeth shuns his former much-respected self, turning into a tyrannical and cruel man.

Macbeth the tyrant

Shakespeare uses the supernatural to influence all the future actions of Macbeth. After the murder of King Duncan and the subsequent murder of Banquo, Macbeth appears to be a man who knows no bounds to his cruelty. The thanes at the court of King Macbeth would naturally look towards Macbeth for leadership, however, his behaviour at the banquet, where he sees the ghost of Banquo, worries the thanes. The fact that the thanes are calling his behaviour madness implies they have no trust or respect in him. As a king, his role does not come easily to him and he decides to seek out the witches for further guidance. Shakespeare's purpose here is to show how much he relies on the witches; how he is guided by them and, more to the point, how he trusts them more than his thanes, and has set spies to watch them:

> "there is not one of them but in his house
> I keep a servant fee'd."

This mistrust in his thanes further adds to his downfall, as he becomes more and more cruel. He has no use of them as advisors, preferring to rely on the witches.

The witches give him further predictions and their apparitions warn him about Macduff. Macbeth's character is unrecognisable as the brave trusted thane as he turns his attention on Lady Macduff and her son. The great warrior has become an oppressor and the deep affection he once had for his wife no longer matters to him. Macbeth keeps knowledge of his murders from Lady Macbeth and appears to dismiss her from any of his plans. As a tyrant, Macbeth has no time for love or human kindness, as shown in his brutal murder of Lady Macduff and her son, as well as in his dismissal of his wife. His ruthless approach to his role as King has endangered all around him.

Macbeth the desperate man

Macbeth's once honourable character has changed beyond recognition by the end of the play. After the battle in Act 1, the Captain reported to King Duncan of Macbeth's greatness. It is significant that Macbeth is not described like this again. The following quote reveals just how little respect the thanes have for Macbeth:

> Menteith: What does the tyrant?
> Caithness: Great Dunsinane he strongly fortifies.
> Some say he's mad, others that lesser hate him
> Do call it valiant fury. [Act 5 Scene 2]

Shakespeare has decided to present the audience with a very complex character in Macbeth. His personality changes dramatically and we are led to believe that it is the intervention of the witches that has caused this dramatic change. It could be argued, however, that the witches simply provide him with the dangerous thoughts, but it is his ambition that overpowers him. Ambition drives him onwards to success but it is also responsible for his failures, as a king, a husband and a friend. He has become desperate in the final scenes and he knows that he is alone and has lost everything. Shakespeare provides us with all the evidence of a great man, rising from an honoured warrior, only to fall into dishonour as a desperate and brutal tyrant, capable of hideous crimes. The fateful ending of his life following his downfall causes both a Jacobean and modern audience to question whether Macbeth's destiny was already determined long before the entrance of the witches.

The importance of Macbeth to the play

Without the character of Macbeth there would be no play, but why has Shakespeare created a monster? The audience knows far more about Macbeth than any other character. His personality is revealed through his wife, his King, Macduff and Malcolm, as well as through Macbeth himself. Shakespeare was a master of characterisation, and Macbeth's character is unravelled, showing both the best and worst sides of it. Shakespeare is able to change the emotions of the audience by creating such a character. Macbeth's blinding ambition is a moral lesson on how the greed and need for power can change someone's personality dramatically. Human nature has many weaknesses and Shakespeare has tapped into these weaknesses through the characters of Macbeth and Lady Macbeth, and it is Shakespeare's skill as a playwright that has created this monster, to entertain and horrify audiences, as well as to warn them of the dangers of passionate, unrivalled ambition.

Lady Macbeth

Lady Macbeth's ambition

Lady Macbeth does not have the complexity of the character of Macbeth, yet it is her ambitious character that forces the action in the early part of the play. Lady Macbeth is trusted and loved by her husband. The letter she receives telling her of the prophecies tells the audience of her ambition to become Queen even in the first act. She speaks to Macbeth about King Duncan's visit:

> "he that is coming
> Must be provided for, and you shall put
> This night's business into my dispatch,"

This quote reveals her ambition and her determination. Lady Macbeth has decided that Macbeth will murder King Duncan. Her need to become Queen appears even stronger than Macbeth's want to become King. It appears she is more ruthless and is certainly prepared to call on supernatural spirits to help her lose her womanly ways, to make her mind strong to help convince her husband to commit murder. Furthermore, it is Lady Macbeth's strong will and her ambition which enable her to take the bloodied daggers from Macbeth and place them with the guards, when Macbeth is paralysed with remorse and fear. However, this pivotal moment also metaphorically places the guilt of the murders into her hands.

Lady Macbeth in control

From the beginning of her interpretation of Macbeth's letter, she is in full control of her actions and calls upon the spirt world to change her personality:

> "Come to my woman's breasts
> And take my milk for gall, you murd'ring ministers."

This quote has demonstrated how she is prepared to give up her role of woman and turn into someone who can control the situation without her female emotions getting in the way. Shakespeare shows that she understands the weaknesses in her husband and that she must be the one who leads the action.

Lady Macbeth has taken on the role of directing the fate of Duncan. The castle becomes her powerhouse as she says:

> "the raven himself is hoarse
> That croaks the fatal entrance of Duncan
> Under my battlements" [Act 1 Scene 5]

The use of the personal pronoun "my" suggests that Lady Macbeth believes the castle belongs to her. This would not be normal behaviour in the time of Shakespeare. Jacobean women would not consider their home belonging to them. They were ruled by their husbands and fathers and had no ownership on any property and titles. Lady Macbeth establishes her authority in this quote, and it demonstrates the strength of her character. Interestingly, Macbeth does not appear to mind his wife taking on this powerful role. Lady Macbeth understands the qualities of her husband; she sees his strength and bravery but she also understands his weakness. She believes him to be too kind-hearted and respecting of others, when she outlines her worries:

> "yet do I fear thy nature,
> It is too full o' the milk of human kindness"

Lady Macbeth uses Macbeth's humanity as a negative trait. It demonstrates her understanding of her husband's character, and of the fact he is a caring man. It is probably one of the last few positive quotes about Macbeth and the fact that she says it negatively demonstrates how controlling she is of the way Macbeth sees himself.

Lady Macbeth plans the murder very carefully and takes full control of the situation, showing she is a woman full of courage and continues to control the murder of Duncan by appealing to the macho side of Macbeth's character with insults regarding his manhood. Lady Macbeth is filled with fury when her husband tells her he cannot go through with the murder:

> "What beast was't then
> That made you break this enterprise to me?
> When you durst do it, then you were a man."

Her words to her husband are brutal and abusive, demonstrating a powerful personality unafraid of her husband. This trait would not be considered part of a woman's personality. Women were expected to show complete respect to their husbands, and Macbeth's decision should have been final. After Macbeth has murdered Duncan and returns with the daggers, it is Lady Macbeth's strong will, and her determination which enables her to take the bloodied daggers from Macbeth and place them with the guards, having smeared blood on their hands and face. The murder of King Duncan is an appalling crime, and yet Lady Macbeth almost dismisses it. She tells Macbeth that: "A little water will clear us of this deed" [Act 2 Scene 2], as if a simple task of washing their hands to clean off the blood of King Duncan will also clean their conscience and guilt of the crime. Lady Macbeth's powerful, influential and controlling nature is the driving force behind the early action of the play.

The downfall of Lady Macbeth

Despite Lady Macbeth's power and her strong-willed determination, Lady Macbeth cannot sustain the control of Macbeth because:

- Macbeth becomes tyrannical and murderous and hides the truth of his murderous plans from his wife.
- It begins to dawn on Lady Macbeth that the murder of King Duncan has changed her husband into a despot that she can barely recognise, let alone control.

As Lady Macbeth experiences these changes, she becomes aware of her part in the terrible events that have occurred. Lady Macbeth could be unshakable with the support and love of her husband, but his behaviour and his lies have frightened her, and her strong will has gone. She feels the guilt over the murder and speaks of the metaphorical blood on her hands as never leaving her:

> "What, will these hands ne'er been clean?
> Here's the smell of blood still; all the perfumes of
> Arabia will not sweeten this little hand."

Lady Macbeth has realised that the murder of Duncan cannot be washed away. Both she and Macbeth have become very different people after their actions. Lady Macbeth has finally comprehended the enormity of what has happened. Her ambition, once great, is now no more. By this point in the play, all her determination has vanished. She is no longer the scheming, controlling and determined woman she once was. Lady Macbeth has been reduced to someone who cannot cope with her husband's behaviour or her own part in the murder and subsequent events. Although her character becomes a figure of pity, she is unlikely to arouse the sympathy of the audience as her earlier behaviour is too shocking and ruthless for the Jacobean audience to accept her weaknesses now.

The importance of Lady Macbeth to the play

Shakespeare has made Lady Macbeth a focal point of the play but his feelings towards women cannot be judged by this. Her behaviour is not that of a normal woman. Lady Macbeth's character in the first part of the play is wicked, evil and manipulative. Shakespeare uses her evil behaviour as a warning to the audience that evil is a wicked personality trait. Her physical weakness at the end of the play shows how over-ambitious tendencies can destroy the compassion and kindness of a person. Shakespeare's purpose in making Lady Macbeth a powerful and ambitious woman is to show her as an example of what power can do if it is given to women. This may be a recognition of Queen Elizabeth the 1st, who was powerful and showed great strength and courage, but unlike Lady Macbeth, her strength did not come from the supernatural but rather her own determination and will. Lady Macbeth seizes her opportunity to become Queen by cunning and persuasive actions and the guilt of her actions brings her downfall. This could suggest that Shakespeare was anti-female, but this is not the case. His concern is more about how supernatural influences can lead to tragedy, and that power, especially in a woman, is dangerous and harmful. There is a warning in Shakespeare's portrayal of Lady Macbeth and her influence over Macbeth which affects the whole play.

King Duncan

Duncan's reputation

King Duncan only appears at the beginning of the play, but he is crucial to the plot. Duncan is a Scottish king with many qualities. He is seen as a just and wise king, who thinks highly of his loyal servants, especially those who have fought against the enemy. He is quick to react to treason and equally quick to praise and honour courage. King Duncan was appointed by God according to the Divine Right of Kings and is respected by his thanes and is seen as a fair and moral ruler. Duncan was a king that the people could admire. In the time of Shakespeare, a king had many enemies who were prepared to murder or harm him. Duncan must trust his subjects unquestionably and if he has any proof that they might be disloyal to him, then he would be expected to act speedily and severely, and therefore must demand the ultimate penalty – death. When the Thane of Cawdor is proved a traitor, Duncan swiftly seals his punishment:

> "Go pronounce his present death
> And with his former title greet Macbeth."

The purpose of introducing the Thane of Cawdor in this way is to demonstrate the generous character of Duncan and also his strength in making decisions. It serves to illustrate the goodness of the King as well as his authority. King Duncan's comment on the former Thane of Cawdor is an ironic statement; he says:

> "he was a gentleman on whom I built
> An absolute trust."

The irony of this comment will serve to be the downfall of Duncan. He trusts his thanes and expects them to be supportive. He had complete trust in the Thane of Cawdor, but this was misplaced. The irony that King Duncan puts his trust in Macbeth, who will become a far greater traitor than the Thane of Cawdor, is not lost on the audience as the play progresses. Shakespeare reminds the audience of Duncan's trustfulness in his subjects and has no idea what will happen to him.

Duncan's fatal error

When King Duncan arrives at Macbeth's castle, he says to Lady Macbeth:

> "Fair and noble hostess,
> We are your guest tonight."

Duncan has made a fatal error of judgement about Lady Macbeth. The word 'noble' would mean honourable and moral, but at this stage, Lady Macbeth is neither fair nor noble. She is plotting the death of Duncan and hides her deceit with a false goodness and gracious behaviour. King Duncan continues his greeting by speaking of Macbeth as someone he respects and loves:

> "We love him highly,
> And shall continue our graces towards him."

King Duncan has dealt with a traitor and is now prepared to honour Macbeth by staying overnight with him. Duncan has no reason but to view the Macbeths in any other way than kind-heartedly and to have complete trust in them. Shakespeare's purpose here is to demonstrate the generosity of the King and to emphasise his good and kind nature. One of Duncan's roles in the play is to serve as a stark contrast to Macbeth's reign. We have the rightful King appointed by God (King Duncan) and the usurper (Macbeth) who takes the throne with no authority from God. Macbeth's reign is cruel and brutal. Shakespeare uses this contrast to emphasise the point of Kingship and how ambition and greed are character traits which will lead to tragedy and have no place in the role of a king.

The importance of King Duncan to the play

Shakespeare has used the character of King Duncan to introduce the qualities of a good king. He is fair and kind, generous and noble. He is used as a contrast to the terrifying reign of Macbeth and serves to show the audience the difference between right and wrong. Again, Shakespeare taps into the character traits of human nature to show that a king can have failings and flaws. King Duncan's weakness appears to be an error of judgement in his fellow men. He trusted the first Thane of Cawdor and he trusted Macbeth, but both characters betrayed him. He is not a complicated character to understand, but the lesson that Shakespeare wants to draw from him is to show that all humans have flaws and must be aware of them if they are to succeed.

The Three Witches

The witches appear four times in the play [Act 1 Scenes 1 and 3, Act 3 Scene 5, and Act 4 Scene 1]. They are highly significant to the plot. Their purpose is to serve as an evil omen of the supernatural and they are able to change the behaviour of Macbeth with their spells and prophecies. In addition to this purpose, Shakespeare would have been aware of King James' interest in the supernatural and the three witches provide intrigue. This would have added to the enjoyment of the play for King James. The witches are introduced at the beginning of the play, [Act 1 Scene 1] deciding when and where to meet Macbeth. This powerful first scene is extremely important as it sets the scene for the play and offers an insight into what might follow. The witches represent omens of evil and the idea of the supernatural would be frightening to the Jacobean audience. The witches provide an introduction to the wickedness that is about to happen through their chant:

> "Fair is foul, and foul is fair:
> Hover through the fog and filthy air."

This quote appears to be a paradox – a contradiction as fair weather cannot, at the same time be foul. It suggests that the witches are responsible for changing the natural order of life into chaos. By bringing the supernatural into the play at the beginning, Shakespeare brings an evil and wickedness to the play. The witches provide Macbeth with the necessary information for him to commit evil.

The responsibility of the witches

The three witches are indirectly responsible for the murder of King Duncan, as well as Macbeth's rise and fall from power. Their predictions are misleading and very dangerous, and appear to fuel the ambition of Macbeth. Shakespeare uses the witches to progress the play by giving the audience an idea of the future and of how their power can influence events. King James would have understood the significance of their charms for Macbeth. King James had not only an interest in witchcraft and charms but a knowledge of how witches and the supernatural were a force of evil. The charm is a spell to feed Macbeth's future ambitions to become more than just a thane. The witches' messages are influential, and Macbeth is drawn to their predictions through a powerful supernatural force. Because of the flaws in Macbeth's character and his ambition, he needs their help to guide him, and the witches, knowing they have him in their power, play to this.

The importance of the three witches to the play

The role of the witches is to give the audience a chance to realise the likelihood of what will happen to Macbeth by their behaviour. They act like a chorus as a means of developing the plot. The witches, however, are far more valuable than this and serve a greater purpose. They create the atmospheric tension, fear and wickedness which is a theme that persists from the beginning to the end of the play. Shakespeare shows that by the end of the play, the witches have served their purpose. They have tricked and manipulated Macbeth into believing that his future is in the hands of fate. His own ambition leads to his downfall, but the witches must accept some of the blame. They are devious and evil and give Macbeth the information to destroy himself and his wife. Shakespeare presents the witches as neither male nor female but rather as supernatural beings who use temptation and magical spells to entice Macbeth to commit wickedness. Unfortunately, the personality of Macbeth means that he cannot resist their prophecies and carries out their wishes exactly as they have planned. Shakespeare uses the witches to reinforce the dangers and evils of witchcraft. Through witchcraft, they are given the power to change good to evil and to lose the faith of God. The witches are dramatic beings and their scheming downfall of Macbeth reminds the audience just how dangerous witchcraft can be.

Banquo

Banquo the man

Banquo is Macbeth's loyal friend and soldier-in-arms. He fought alongside Macbeth to help win the battle which earned Macbeth and himself the grateful respect of the King. His role in the play contrasts with Macbeth. He also receives prophecies from the witches, but his understanding is greater than Macbeth's and he does not respond with the same feelings and is not tempted to act upon the predictions. He is cleverly created by Shakespeare to act as a dramatic foil for Macbeth – he is what Macbeth could have become.

Banquo's reaction to the witches

Banquo shows no signs of indulging in the prophecies of the witches. He does not react in the same way as Macbeth. Banquo is a measured and calm man and his reaction to the witches' prophecies regarding him and his children does not cause the "evil desires" that Macbeth appears to feel. He does, however, have concerns "the instruments of darkness tell us truths" but he feels this will bring harm rather than good. Banquo is loyal and a good friend of Macbeth; he warns Macbeth about trusting in the prophecies, but Macbeth does not listen to him. At this point Banquo's role in the play is to show him as a man who is not only brave, but as someone who is mindful to the feelings of others and he has a clear realisation that the witches have had an influential effect on Macbeth which may lead to evil. After Macduff has revealed the horrors of Duncan's murder, Banquo is shocked and pledges:

> "To the great hand of God, I stand and thence
> Against the undivulg'd pretence I fight
> Of treasonous malice."

The purpose of the quote is to show that Banquo is putting himself into God's hands and his plan is to seek out and avenge this terrible murder. It shows the influence of the Divine Right of Kings, whereby Banquo believes that it is only God who can take the life of a king and knows that this death is a tyrannous plot.

The importance of Banquo to the play

Shakespeare has created the character of Banquo as someone who is both brave and a thane. He is a warrior like Macbeth but stands for integrity and loyalty. This contrast with Macbeth is a deliberate ploy by Shakespeare to reinforce how greed and ambition can change a person. Despite both Macbeth and Banquo being very similar at the beginning of the play, Banquo's faith in God is not shaken by the predictions of the witches. He does not have the fatal flaw in his personality that causes the downfall of Macbeth, but he does possess a weakness. He feels suspicious of Macbeth and thinks he "played'st most foully" [Act 3 Scene 1] to become King. Ironically, his trustfulness and his loyalty to Macbeth prevent him from voicing his suspicions and his loyalty costs him his life. Macbeth has Banquo murdered because he sees Banquo as a threat to his crown.

Shakespeare uses the murder of Banquo to help bring about the downfall of Macbeth. By appearing as a ghost, Banquo causes great distress to Macbeth, giving the thanes reason to be concerned about Macbeth's behaviour and the state of his mind. Banquo's ghost helps the audience to consider the brutality of Macbeth and to emphasise the sense of the supernatural.

Macduff

Macduff the man

Macduff was born by caesarean section* and is the only person able to kill Macbeth. This fact alone makes him an important character in the play. At the beginning of the play Macduff is portrayed as honourable and responsible. Trusted to wake Duncan at an early hour, he discovers Duncan's murder and is horrified. Clearly the murder has shocked him, and he cannot quite believe that the King could be killed in such a way. He is a loyal thane, who respected and loved King Duncan.

Macduff's reaction to Macbeth

Macduff doesn't attend Macbeth's coronation at Scone. This act in itself can be seen as bold defiance from a thane who was loyal to King Duncan. It can also be viewed as an insult to the newly crowned King. The reaction of Macduff towards Macbeth is in stark contrast to his reaction at the death of King Duncan. Macduff, when asked by Ross whether he will go to Scone answers, "No, cousin, I'll to Fife". He also adds the comment: "Well may you see things well done there. Adieu. Lest our old robes sit easier than our new". This comment can be interpreted as Macbeth's new robes, meaning his kingly robes, may not suit him as well as his old robes, specifically the clothes he wore as a thane and nobleman. It is clear from the outset that Macduff is suspicious of Macbeth and his part in the death of Duncan.

Macduff's judgement

Macduff, like Banquo, has always been a trusty and honourable servant to King Duncan, but he makes a bad judgement, as his decision to leave his wife and son alone costs him dearly. He leaves his wife and child and goes to England, which suggests irresponsibility, but it could also be seen as a brave action as his motives are to rally Malcolm to fight Macbeth. The mark of a good thane was putting King and country before everything and this seems to have been the reason for his decision to go to England.

Macduff's slaying of Macbeth

After he hears of his wife and son's death, Macduff decides to seek out Macbeth with a single purpose – to kill him. On finding Macbeth he says:

> "I have no words;
> My voice is my sword, thou bloodier villain
> Than terms can give thee out."

The word 'terms' means words; he wishes his sword to speak for him. His determination and strength can be felt in this quote. Having killed Macbeth and beheaded him, Macduff acknowledges Malcolm as the true King:

> "Hail, King, for so thou art. Beholds where stands
> The usurper's cursed head. The time is free."

Macduff's true feelings are important to the audience as a final reminder that Macbeth was not the chosen King but a usurper – someone who achieved the crown through evil actions. Unlike Macbeth, he killed the current King, not for his own selfish gains, but for the greater good of Scotland.

The importance of Macduff to the play

Macduff is an interesting character as he appears both brave and weak. Shakespeare reveals him as having the courage not to attend Macbeth's coronation which shows independence. Shakespeare shows him as a character who has humanity and feels genuine pain as he grieves for his murdered wife and son. There is a contrast here between himself and Macbeth. Macbeth barely acknowledges his wife's death. When thinking about Macduff it is useful to consider his actions. Is he a traitor leaving the court of Macbeth, or noble in his quest to fight against Macbeth and establish the true King of Scotland? Macduff is honest and has a great love for his country. His comment to Malcolm leaves the audience in no doubt as to how he feels about how Macbeth has wounded his country: "Bleed, bleed, poor country". Macduff is a man of great passion; Shakespeare has created Macduff for a purpose: to kill Macbeth. He is predestined to do so as he was "not born of woman" [Act 5 Scene 3]. He is used by Shakespeare as the only person who will be able to kill Macbeth and, as a consequence, has an important role in the play.

Minor Characters

Malcolm

Malcolm is the eldest son of Duncan and is chosen by Duncan to become the next King after Duncan's death. Because he is fearful of his own destiny after his father's murder, he escapes to England. This may be a weakness in his character, but perhaps it shows wisdom as well. Malcolm fears for his life after the death of his father and seeks refuge in the royal court in England. He appears at the end of the play when Macduff seeks him out and is ready to oppose Macbeth.

Shakespeare's purpose in creating Malcolm as the rightful King of Scotland is to use him as a contrast to Macbeth. Malcolm shows innocence. He is not as corrupt as Macbeth. He reflects on King Edward in England, and lists his virtues, showing how much King Edward differs from Macbeth. He is modest of his own opinion on whether he will make a good king. Shakespeare allows Malcolm to have a 'voice' regarding the state of Scotland:

> "I think our country sinks beneath the yoke;
> It weeps, it bleeds, and each new day a gash
> Is added to her wounds."

Shakespeare has used symbolism in this quote. The country of Scotland has been personified as a human being which has been wounded, and the wounding continues. It typifies the theme of blood and corruption. Malcolm's mention of disease and illness of the country ruled by Macbeth is important to the play. It is particularly important to the audience as they would fully understand how Macbeth has destroyed the country. Countries were seen as a 'body' with the King at the head of the body. If the King was sick in mind, or evil and tyrannous, then the whole body was infected. Shakespeare's purpose in giving the character of Malcolm such insight is to remind the audience how a tyrannous king or 'head' of a country can change the country and destroy it.

Ross

Ross is a thane and, like the others, is loyal to King Duncan. He is created to bring news to various people in the play, which in turn informs the audience of what is happening. For example, in Act 1 Scene 3, it is Ross who brings the news of the King to Macbeth:

> "And in earnest of a greater honour,
> He bade me, from him, call thee Thane of Cawdor:
> In which addition, hail most worthy thane,
> For it is thine."

Here, Ross' role establishes how the King has reacted to Macbeth's bravery and to confirm the prophecies of the witches. In Act 4 Scene 3, Ross brings the news to Macduff of the terrible murder of his wife and children:

> "Your castle is surpris'd: your wife and babes
> Savagely slaughter'd. To relate the manner,
> Were on the quarry of these murder'd deer
> To add the death of you."

The use of sibilance makes the murders even more terrible and suggests sinister actions. 'Deer' is a play on the word 'dear' but also suggests that the bodies are piled upon each other, similar to hunting deer. Ross brings important news and he also joins the other thanes who turn against Macbeth.

Progress and Revision Check

1. How is Macbeth presented at the beginning of the play?
2. How does Macbeth react to the three prophecies of the witches?
3. How does Lady Macbeth persuade Macbeth that he must murder King Duncan? What does this tell us about Macbeth's character?
4. What is Macbeth's character like at the end of the play?
5. Why does Lady Macbeth wish to change her personality and character traits at the beginning of the play?
6. What do the witches represent in the play?
7. How does Banquo differ from Macbeth in his personality?
8. How would a Jacobean audience react to the murdering of Macduff's family?
9. How does Macduff feel about Macbeth at the end of the play and what is his plan?
10. Why does Macbeth revert to his earlier characteristics at the very end of the play?

~ THEMES ~

Ambition

One of the strongest themes in the play is ambition. Not only is it the driving force of Macbeth's and Lady Macbeth's behaviour, but it is taken from the classical Greek tragedies of *Hubris*, the downfall (and ultimate death) of the hero through his overreaching ambition.

Ambition and the corruption of Macbeth

For *Macbeth* to be a true tragedy it was necessary for the hero, a well-respected, loyal and honest man to become too vain and filled with his own ambition to such an extent that it leads to his downfall and ultimate death. As a general in the army and a noble warrior, one might expect Macbeth to have ambition for promotion, but not to the extent where Macbeth uses it to justify cold-blooded killing and tyrannical rule. Macbeth wants to become King and this ambition drives him forward to murder anyone who he feels is a threat to his rule. As his position becomes stronger and the need for power becomes greater, Macbeth appears to have little understanding of his own behaviour and as the play progresses, his ambition drives him forward relentlessly. At the beginning of the play Macbeth says:

> "I have no spur
> To prick the sides of my intent, but only
> Vaulting ambition, which o'erleaps itself,
> And falls on the other–"

This is the only time Macbeth understands the reality of his behaviour. Shakespeare's use of the personification 'vaulting' suggests that Macbeth's ambition is a living being and the warning that it falls on the other side evokes a powerful image of how great ambition can cause a downfall in the fortunes of a person. When Macbeth allows his ambitions to overtake his level-headedness, he becomes corrupt. This corruption is due to his complete disregard for anyone else and his lack of respect for the duties and qualities of a king. Even when he becomes King, he cannot accept that he has achieved his ambition and continues in his violent ways until the end of the play. Macbeth becomes increasingly desperate and continues with his senseless killing of innocent people, allowing his ambition to take over his life. Ambition appears to be the fatal flaw in Macbeth's character and therefore it is this ambition which is responsible for his downfall.

Ambition and the corruption of Lady Macbeth

Lady Macbeth is as ambitious as her husband, perhaps more so, and ensures he follows her direction in the murder of Duncan. She has a greater determination than Macbeth to pursue her own ambitions. Unlike Macbeth however, Lady Macbeth is not able to endure the consequences of her sinful behaviour. Her first display of ambition is after she receives the letter from Macbeth in Act 1 Scene 5. She is delighted with the witches' prophecies and prepares herself for action through the supernatural. Her willingness to discard her own morals is shown in this quote:

> "Make thick my blood.
> Stop up the access and passage to remorse."

The imperative 'make' is a command to the spirits. Lady Macbeth is commanding them to act. The metaphorical meaning here is that she wishes not to feel regret for what she is about to do. Lady Macbeth has allowed her own morals of kindness and goodness to be cast aside and she wants to feel no guilt after she carries out her plan. This establishes the lengths she is prepared to go to, to achieve her ambition. It also exposes Lady Macbeth's attitude about power; she feels that the only way to achieve greatness is to ignore what is right and wrong.

The contrast between Lady Macbeth and her husband may lead the audience to believe that her ambition is the greater of the two, but later in the play it is Macbeth whose ambition grows strong whilst Lady Macbeth's grows weak. Lady Macbeth's ambition appears to affect her more than it does Macbeth, but equally her guilt of the crime affects her more strongly than her husband. Her ambition leaves her as she realises the enormity of what she has done and her final act is to commit suicide. Like Macbeth, Lady Macbeth's ambition leads to her downfall.

Shakespeare's purpose for the theme of ambition

Shakespeare uses ambition as a weakness rather than a strength in the protagonists' characters. Macbeth kills King Duncan against his better judgement and the consequences of this are tragic. Ambitious people usually do well and prosper but if ambition is taken too far and begins to control the thoughts and actions of the person, then it can be seen as a weakness and can lead (in the case of Macbeth) to tragedy. Macbeth, having achieved his ambition to become King, feels powerful and needs to keep this power by organising the deaths of his friend, Banquo and other characters that he perceives as a threat. His original ambition to become King has been lost in his quest for greatness. He mistakes ambition for desire and continues with this, encouraged by the prophecies of the witches to drive himself forward until he becomes out of control. Shakespeare uses both Macbeth and Lady Macbeth to show just how corrupt ambition can be. Macbeth appears to be poisoned by his ambition and this leads to shame, dishonour and ultimately death. This dishonour leaves Macbeth with no trusted friends and many enemies. Shakespeare has also made Lady Macbeth corrupted by her ambition. She slips into madness and her guilt is so great that she takes her own life.

Shakespeare alerts the audience to the evils of driving ambition and the dangers of ignoring the wisdom of God.

Fate

Fate may seem a strange theme to consider because Macbeth's actions are driven by his own ambition and that of Lady Macbeth. Fate is something that is already predestined, and it is worth considering whether Macbeth's fate had already been decided. The word 'fate' can refer to the development of events and actions which are outside the control of a person. Therefore, the fate of Macbeth is governed by the supernatural powers of the witches and they determine his future.

The fate of Macbeth

Macbeth's meeting with the witches has been arranged in the first scene by the witches, when they agree exactly when, where and who to meet:

> "Where's the place?
> Upon the heath
> There to meet with Macbeth."

Is the seal of fate already decided for Macbeth at this early stage of the play? Although Macbeth could have dismissed their predictions, they give him the belief that he can become King and they also tell him that he will become the new Thane of Cawdor. This is confirmed when, no sooner has he left the witches, than the prophecy of him becoming the Thane of Cawdor becomes a reality; Ross, sent by the King, brings Macbeth news of the title. Given that the witches told Macbeth of the three events and two have been honoured, it is not surprising that Macbeth thinks of the third as being an accurate prediction. Macbeth puts absolute trust in the fate that the witches have predicted for him. He believes that this is to be his destiny and cannot be changed. The meeting of the witches is not due to chance, as they have already decided the fate of Macbeth in Act 1 Scene 1. His absolute belief in their words seals his fate and he rejects his own morals in order to make their prophecies a reality. As a consequence of this, Macbeth kills those he does not trust or who offer any barriers to him achieving all that the witches have offered. This leads the audience to question whether it was his fate to be this evil all along.

The fate of Lady Macbeth

Lady Macbeth suffers a similar fate to her husband. She has great ambition for her husband to be King and for herself to be Queen. How much of her fate is determined by the witches is hard to know. It could be said that because of Macbeth's predictions, from his meeting with the witches, Lady Macbeth's fate is sealed. Lady Macbeth calls on supernatural powers to help her. The witches have offered Macbeth a new life by altering his fate through trickery. Macbeth has passed this pre-arranged fate on to his wife. At any point, she could have tried to dissuade her husband as their relationship was very strong and her ability to persuade Macbeth, would have probably changed his mind, but she is tempted by the fate of the witches as much as him.

The fate of Banquo and Duncan

Although Banquo does not react to the prophecies of the witches and has no reason to take them seriously, the witches may have also, ironically, sealed the fate of Banquo, via Macbeth. The witches' words to Banquo offer even more promise than to Macbeth:

> "Lesser than Macbeth, and greater.
> Not so happy, yet much happier.
> Thou shalt get kings, though thou be none."

These words appear to be a riddle and contradiction. How can Banquo be not so happy but much happier? The significance of these words is to show that there is menace and magic in the meaning and the meaning can be interpreted in different ways. By telling Banquo that his heirs will become future kings does not appear to impress Banquo, however Macbeth realises that to become King, Macbeth must rid himself of all potential threats and therefore, this includes getting rid of Banquo.

Duncan's fate is also going to change with Macbeth and Banquo's meeting of the witches. In order for Macbeth to prove the prophecies true, he must rid himself of the King. It is ironic that Duncan never meets the witches, but his fate is set because of their predictions.

Shakespeare's purpose for the theme of fate

Shakespeare wants us to believe that Macbeth has two choices: the choice of the witches to go along with their prophecies or to reject them and let the future happen naturally. We do not know what the future holds, but by the intervention of supernatural powers, the future becomes predetermined. Shakespeare invites the audience to question the difference between fate and free will. Has Macbeth really got two choices? Or have the witches determined his path? Banquo, in contrast to Macbeth, has no trust in the words of the witches and dismisses them. He has also been offered information which could lead him to pursue the crown in order to ensure his son becomes King. Banquo, however, rejects the witches' predictions, which suggests that both Macbeth and Banquo have been given choices and they both choose different routes. It is ironic that Banquo, despite his rejection of the witches, and his choice to let normal events take him through life, still cannot escape his fate.

The Supernatural

The theme of the supernatural is prominent in the play. From the very beginning the witches are described as supernatural beings. They are capable of magic and deception and can summon the spirits as well as make spells which cause Macbeth's hallucinations. Interfering with the supernatural may bring evil to whoever meddles with it. It is far safer for Macbeth to ignore the witches, but their presence is strong and their prophecies powerful and addictive. The supernatural is the dark force which continues from the meeting of the witches to the end of the play.

The supernatural and its effect on Macbeth

Macbeth meets the witches for the first time and he becomes strongly influenced by the unnatural forces. At first, he questions them:

> "Say from whence
> You owe this strange intelligence, or why
> Upon the blasted heath you stop our way
> With such prophetic greeting?"

Initially, Macbeth questions the motives of the supernatural. But as some of the predictions become immediately true, he believes what they predict. Before his murder of Duncan, he begins to question what is real. His hallucination of the dagger which appears in front of him, suggests that dark forces are at play. The dagger appears as a hallucination but although its presence is not real, there seems to be an evil emitting from the dagger to lead Macbeth forward to murder the King:

> "Art thou not, fatal vision, sensible
> To feeling as to sight? Or art thou but
> A dagger of the mind"

The adjective 'fatal' is used to full effect as a dagger will end the life of Duncan. A 'dagger of the mind' can refer simply to a dagger in Macbeth's imagination, but it suggests that the supernatural has entered his consciousness and is beginning to trick his senses.

Macbeth's confusion is created by the powers of the supernatural. The evil of the supernatural plays on his mind again when he sees the vision of Banquo's ghost. A supernatural being which can only be seen by Macbeth – is it another illusion of his mind or a real ghost? He asks the ghost of Banquo to "Avaunt and quit my sight! Let the earth hide thee!" In this quote, Macbeth is commanding the ghost to leave his sight. Again, there is a question about what is real and what is false. He needs the vision to disappear and says: "Let the earth hide thee". Banquo is buried in the earth and cannot rise; Macbeth pleads with the ghost to go back there but interestingly, it is only Macbeth that can see this apparition. Shakespeare uses this is as a direct reference to the ghostlike, mystical beings belonging to hell. Mortals lived above ground, the spirits were unnatural and dwelled elsewhere. The fact that no one else can see the ghost is significant, as the whole idea of the supernatural may be imaginary. There is no good to be had in believing in the supernatural. It is a power of evil that will result in destruction. Macbeth finds out too late that his trust in the witches is false and his fate is determined by his own actions.

The supernatural and its effect on Lady Macbeth

Macbeth is not the only character who summons the supernatural: Lady Macbeth calls on them in Act 1 Scene 5:

> "Come you spirits
> That tend on mortal thoughts, unsex me here"

Lady Macbeth uses the imperative 'come' to demand action. She is openly inviting the spirits to change her personality. 'Unsex me here' is another invitation for the spirit world to affect her. The verb 'unsex' is referring to her womanly ways, her goodness and humanity. She needs to dismiss these qualities to ensure she can carry out her plan, which is a dangerous command that would have disturbed the audience. Her call to the spirits is unnatural and she asks them to help her become determined and brave and to fill her with "direst cruelty", hoping that the supernatural powers can transform her from the fair and gentle lady of the castle, a respectful hostess and a loving wife, to someone with the spirit and bravery and cold-hearted passion of a man. She is inviting danger and evil to allow her to become resolute in her quest. Shakespeare's purpose here is to show how powerful and cunning Lady Macbeth has become through the supernatural influences. It appears that Lady Macbeth has also become addicted to the power of the supernatural and, like Macbeth, has become blinded by it.

The supernatural and its effect on Banquo

Banquo sees the witches at the same time as Macbeth, but they appear to have no effect on him. He questions the visitation of the witches and wonders whether they (Macbeth and Banquo) "have eaten of the insane root". Hemlock was thought to cause madness, which could make someone believe in hallucinations. The fact that Banquo comments on this, shows his rational mind has won against the supernatural influences. He is looking for a reason for the witches' existence and believes that he and Macbeth must have been given a drug in the form of hemlock for their visions. Shakespeare creates the character of Macbeth to have a fatal flaw and because of this characteristic, it is only Macbeth who will be troubled by the witches and their powers, not Banquo.

The supernatural and its effect on nature

The supernatural is an alarming and frightful presence which is also presented through the weather. Whenever the supernatural appears the weather is chaotic. For example, the killing of Duncan happens on a very dark and starless night. This feels distressing and frightening. Lennox describes the night as:

> "The night has been unruly: where we lay,
> Our chimneys were blown down, and, as they say,
> Lamentings heard i' th' air, strange screams of death."

These words said by Lennox refer to both the weather and the supernatural. The 'strange screams of death' could come from the supernatural but are more likely to symbolise that there is evil on earth. The wind, an omen of evil, appears strong enough to blow down chimneys, which is an example of how the supernatural disrupts the world. The word 'lamentings' suggests mournful howling, again foretelling the horrors that have been committed. This description of the weather would add fear to the already superstitious Jacobean audience.

Shakespeare's purpose for the theme of the supernatural

Shakespeare purpose in using the supernatural as a theme is to show how dangerous it is to believe in witchcraft and the supernatural, and how it can be used to trick the mind into believing that it is a real force. King James was very interested in the supernatural and the theme is deliberately powerful throughout the play. King James was aware of witches' powers and hated them. Many women were accused of witchcraft, simply because they used herbs to make up potions to heal the sick. However, the witches in *Macbeth* are far more forceful and create a fearful anxiety in both Macbeth and the audience. The supernatural is not a natural phenomenon* and Shakespeare has used it in *Macbeth* to demonstrate wickedness. The mystical and eerie effect it has on the characters can help change their behaviour, but it cannot be responsible for their actions. Only Macbeth can make the decision to murder Duncan. His wife can use all her persuasive powers to guide him, and the witches can entice him with their prophecies, but ultimately it is his decision. Fate has played a hand in this choice, but it is Macbeth who stabs Duncan. Shakespeare also uses the supernatural to foreshadow events and this in turn adds tension and dramatic purpose. The events that will follow are told by the witches in the form of predictions. They help the audience understand what is about to happen and are used by Shakespeare as signs of what is to come. The view that Shakespeare presents to the audience is that the supernatural is both unnatural and evil.

Revenge

Revenge is a powerful theme in the play. At the time of Shakespeare, revenge was a form of retribution, payback for an injustice. It was a method of justice for wrongdoings and was a necessary action in the eyes of a Jacobean audience.

Macbeth and revenge

After the murder of Duncan, Macbeth is seen to take hasty revenge on Duncan's guards. He kills them immediately. This is an ironic revenge, as the guards were innocent, but Macbeth hopes the thanes would see it as justified, as the crime was so shocking the revenge should be instant:

> "O, yet I do repent me of my fury,
> That I did kill them."

His words suggest that he is repentant of his quick actions. It is interesting to note that no one criticises Macbeth for this action, as it is a form of immediate revenge taking an 'eye for an eye'. Also, the guards are of a lower order than Macbeth in the hierarchy and his friends and the audience are unlikely to see this as murder but as a necessary revenge. Of course, the act is to cover up the real murder of Duncan and although this rouses suspicion with Macduff and the King's two sons, it would have been an acceptable killing for those unaware that Macbeth had murdered the King.

Other characters and revenge

The theme of revenge affects many of the characters. For example, Duncan, a wise and just king, takes revenge on the original Thane of Cawdor. Duncan's demand for the execution of the tyrannous thane was used as a form of justice:

> "No more that the Thane of Cawdor shall deceive
> Our bosom interest"

The audience learn later that this is an ironic statement as Macbeth is more of a traitor than the Thane of Cawdor can ever be. Shakespeare's purpose in introducing the theme of revenge through Duncan is to allow the audience to see that revenge in the right hands can be justified but in the wrong hands is dangerous. There are other instances of revenge in the play:

- Both Malcolm and Donaldbain seek revenge for the murder of their father, but this revenge does not materialise until later in the play.
- Banquo also pursues vengeance by appearing firstly as a ghost and later after Macbeth has seen the apparitions of the eight kings: "for the blood-bolter's Banquo smiles upon on me". This suggests that Banquo has got his revenge and the smile is a mocking smile.

There is a wider system of revenge in the play. Macbeth is killed and therefore the audience, as well as his subjects get their revenge for his tyrannical and cruel behaviour and his cold-blooded murder of innocent women and children. Macduff seeks his revenge in the murder of Macbeth. Again, the audience would have felt relieved that he had his retribution for the loss of his family.

Shakespeare's purpose for the theme of revenge

Shakespeare's purpose in introducing the theme of revenge is to reinforce its classical meaning of the word. The word 'revenge' comes from the Greek goddess of revenge whose name was Nemesis. Nemesis was the goddess of fate, divine retribution and revenge. She could bring punishment on behalf of those who had been unfairly wronged. Duncan, Banquo and Macduff had all been unfairly wronged by the actions of Macbeth and he must be punished for these actions. Therefore, Macbeth meets his Nemesis for all his evil doings by his eventual death. Shakespeare also shows the differences between revenge and justice.

Parallel contrasts such as goodness and evil, revenge and justice, supernatural and the natural are used throughout the play. Macbeth, by his cruel murders, has left many of the characters seeking revenge: Donaldbain, Malcolm, and Fleance all lose their fathers. Seyward and Macduff lose their sons, and in the case of Macduff, he also loses his wife. Their revenge is seen as justifiable by the audience as Macbeth has murdered their family members out of ambition and greed.

Brutality and Violence

Macbeth is a violent, brutal and bloody play. It begins in battle and contains the murder of men, women, and children. Shakespeare wrote many plays of tragedy and history which highlighted the brutality of the time, and the brutality of events that have happened throughout history. In Act 1 Scene 2, Shakespeare uses the metaphor "unseam'd him from the nave to th'chaps" to describe how Macbeth killed his enemy. This quote uses a metaphorical idea that MacDonald was unseam'd as if undoing a seam on clothing. In fact, it is much more brutal than this. Macbeth ripped him apart by splitting him open from his stomach to his jaw. This brutality was then concluded with Macbeth chopping off the head of MacDonald and spearing it on the battlements. This description is used by Shakespeare to show how brave and fearless Macbeth had been during the battle, but also to show that there was almost a satisfaction in the killing. Opening the play with this image sets the scene for further brutality to come.

The brutality and violence of Macbeth

The brutal way that Macbeth murdered Duncan in a particularly violent frenzy, with Duncan being stabbed to death by several strikes of the daggers, suggests a ruthless and vicious killing. The theme of brutality in Macbeth's character is then continued with the death of Banquo. He is murdered by the hired killers of Macbeth, but the brutality of Macbeth's instructions to them is very clear: For the murderers to carry out Macbeth's instructions, they must hide and kill Banquo in a surprise attack. Macbeth has ordered both Banquo and Fleance to be killed; he shows no mercy for the young innocent boy. He praises the murderers as "the best o' th' cutthroats". This quote demonstrates how Macbeth values the merciless killing, praising the men for their cruelty. His brutality used in war has been transferred to innocent people. Macbeth decides that the wife and children of Macduff must be killed and again shows no humanity in the killing. Macbeth has become a cruel tyrant; his acts of unmerciful killing are simply to secure his crown. At the end of the play Macbeth is described as a "butcher". This metaphor suggests the idea of slaughter in the minds of the audience, which is exactly how Macbeth carried out his killings and accurately summarises how brutal Macbeth has been throughout the play.

Shakespeare's purpose in using the theme of brutality and violence

Shakespeare's purpose in using the theme of brutality throughout the play is to demonstrate how Macbeth's use of brutality becomes a way of life and this violence on the stage is used to manipulate the audience. Any possible sympathy that the audience may feel towards Macbeth would disappear the more that Macbeth kills. It was expected that in war there would be bloodshed, but as Macbeth proceeds to kill one character after another, he shows cruel violence and horrifying brutality. He changes from being the brave general, killing people in the name of his King to a cruel murderer of the innocent and his acts of violence become increasingly desperate. Macbeth loses his ability to recognise just how violent his murders have become.

Shakespeare is not using this violence unnecessarily but to show how evil, through the supernatural, has become the way of life for Macbeth. The Jacobean audience would have watched the play in horror as these acts of murder were so graphic. Macbeth the warrior is not evil; he kills his enemies because this is what happens in war. However, Macbeth the tyrant is essentially evil, and Shakespeare makes a clear division of the two, through his acts of brutality.

Kingship

Kingship is about the rule of Kings. The King was the Head of State and Head of the Church. It was believed in the times of Shakespeare that God had power to create and destroy life. God could give life or take it away. The King, as God's representative on earth, could also spare a life or pronounce someone's death. Whatever a king decided to do, he was unaccountable to anyone but God. The King could rule his people well or badly; he could be cruel or kind and he had loyal subjects who believed he was in the place of God and represented God to the people. Many of his actions were accepted unconditionally but whilst he may have enemies, his power was such that he could bring absolute justice to anyone he saw as a traitor. King James ruled with this guideline and therefore would be aware of how Macbeth had abused this authority.

Duncan's representation of kingship

King Duncan was a king with great kindness, as well as being a fair and just ruler. Macbeth acknowledges this, even when he is contemplating to kill him:

> "this Duncan
> Hath borne his faculties so meek, hath been
> So clear in his great office, that his virtues
> Will plead like angels"

Shakespeare uses this quote to show the qualities of King Duncan, and Macbeth's acknowledgement of these qualities. King Duncan was noble, just and kind. He was moral and humble in his time as King. Macbeth feels that King Duncan had faultless virtues and questions how he could possibly take his life.

Macbeth's representation of kingship

Once Macbeth has committed the murder of Duncan and claimed himself King, he is presented as cruel, weak and evil. His actions are motivated by his need to become King. It is ironic that Macbeth is aware of just how good King Duncan has been. He praises Duncan for being "meek" (not arrogant) and clear in his role as King, knowing how to behave and how to rule. By allowing the supernatural to influence his decisions, Macbeth has effectively dismissed God. He does not rule by any of the laws that belong to the idea of the Divine Right of Kings. After Macbeth accepts the predictions of the witches, he reigns with his own rules. Macbeth is filled with confidence, but at the same time, he is filled with fear. He still needs to rid himself of his enemies, their wives, children and future children. He destroys the protection that the Scottish people felt under King Duncan and has lost the respect of his thanes. His ruling of the country is tyrannous and evil. He is considered a usurper of the crown and a wicked and dangerous ruler. The respect which is expected by the royal subjects does not exist for Macbeth. His kingship is seen as tyrannical and even his most loyal thanes question his sanity. Macbeth continues this tyrannical rule throughout the play until his death. His kingship is consistently weak and causes great harm to those around him.

Shakespeare's purpose for the theme of kingship

Shakespeare uses the theme of kingship to reinforce the idea of the Divine Right of Kings. King Duncan was crowned King according to God and acted as his representative on earth. The ideal king is someone who represents order and justice. A good king could also reward his subjects and show affection and kindness. The difference between a good king and a bad one is that a good king would put his country before his own interests. Macbeth represents the opposite of this. Not only is he tyrannical but he puts his own ambitions above his country and the country falls into chaos. Malcolm outlines the qualities of a good king:

> "I have none. The King – becoming graces–
> As justice, verity, temp'rance, stableness,
> Bounty, perseverance, mercy, lowliness,
> Devotion, patience, courage, fortitude–"

Malcolm lists the virtues of King Edward of England and these virtues reflect both the virtues of Duncan and of King James. The contrast between King Edward and King Macbeth could not have been greater. Shakespeare's ultimate purpose in introducing this theme was to show respect for King James and remind the audience just how dangerous a king like Macbeth is, which would protect the position of King James.

Progress and Revision Check

1. How does Macbeth respond to the witches' prophecies?
2. How does Lady Macbeth's ambition establish itself in the play?
3. To what extent does fate play a part in Macbeth's downfall?
4. What is the effect of the supernatural on the weather and how is this relevant to the play?
5. Why is Banquo's ghost important to reinforce the idea of the supernatural?
6. Why is it justified that Macduff takes revenge on Macbeth?
7. In Jacobean beliefs, when can revenge be justified?
8. Why does Shakespeare use such violence in describing the reign of Macbeth?
9. What are the main qualities a good king should have?
10. Why is the theme of kingship important to the play as a whole?

~ FORM, STRUCTURE AND LANGUAGE ~

Form

The form of *Macbeth* is in the style of a dramatic play, specifically a tragedy. Tragedy came from the Ancient Greek drama, whereby there were certain key features recognised in this form of drama. There had to be a protagonist (the central character) who was of some importance, perhaps of noble birth or even royalty. During the play, this protagonist would reveal a fatal flaw in his or her character, which would cause unhappiness and often death. A fatal flaw means a weakness or fault in someone's personality. The Greek tragedy revolved around one location and a short time scale. Shakespeare adapted this form, but the time scale and location have been developed. The time scale of *Macbeth* is over a longer period, and the location moves from Scotland to England and then back to Dunsinane Castle. In the play, Macbeth is clearly the protagonist and his fatal flaw is ambition. He is of noble birth, a good and brave man but his need for power results in his death. Although the plot has conventional qualities of tragedy, it could be argued that Lady Macbeth also suffers from her overambitious plans and suffers a similar fate to Macbeth, in as much as she falls from grace and suffers a great downfall. Even though Shakespeare enhanced the form for dramatic purposes, the genre of tragedy is completely realised and *Macbeth* remains one of the greatest tragedies ever written.

Structure

Chronological structure

Macbeth has a chronological structure, which means that events in the play happen one after another. Not all the events are acted on stage, for example the murder of Duncan is instead revealed through the actors' dramatic words. Shakespeare builds on his structure of the play to highlight various scenes and actions, for example:

- The intervention of the witches at the beginning of the play is critical to this structure as it is used as a starting point for all of Macbeth's actions.
- The ending of the play not only concludes *Macbeth* effectively but also offers the audience a satisfactory resolution to the fundamental plot of the play, which is based around ambition and fall, good and evil, action and consequence.

The stages of *Macbeth* are well defined. We can consider each stage to see how the play develops.

Stage 1

This is usually known as the exposition of the play. The exposition means the beginning of the play where the main characters, the location and the weather are introduced. There is a positive view of both Duncan and Macbeth, one as a great king and the other as a great warrior. It also sets out the main ideas of murder and ambition through the introduction of the witches and their predictions.

Stage 2

A number of related events occur: the letter to Lady Macbeth, Macbeth's indecision about whether he should murder the King, the visit of King Duncan, and finally the persuasion and control of Lady Macbeth which leads to the murder of King Duncan. This murder brings the critical action that will ultimately be the downfall of Macbeth.

Stage 3

This stage demonstrates a pivotal turning point where Macbeth's fortunes change by his own actions. He becomes fearful of anyone that may become a threat to his kingship. The Macbeths have achieved their wishes; Macbeth becomes King and there appear to be no consequences to their actions. But very soon events change rapidly for Macbeth as he arranges the brutal murders of Banquo and Fleance. His tyrannical and unpredictable behaviour has changed him.

Stage 4

This stage brings together a number of actions:

- Macduff's family are slaughtered which provides an opponent to Macbeth in the form of Macduff.
- Macbeth needs to visit the witches again to take comfort and confidence from their predictions.

Shakespeare has used dramatic irony* to show how Macbeth cannot interpret the symbols of the apparitions conjured up by the witches, but the audience is fully aware of what is happening and understand the real meanings of the apparitions. This is a necessary aspect of the structure of the play as Macbeth's absolute belief in the witches' predictions continues.

Stage 5

This stage not only concludes the play, but the scenes are structured to ensure that the tension and drama are built up to the climax of the play and the final tragedy. The concluding scenes demonstrate continuous action between Macbeth and his enemies. In a dramatic climax, Macbeth is slain by Macduff. Shakespeare has concluded the play with the final downfall of Macbeth and Lady Macbeth. Good rises above evil and the moral meaning of this statement was not lost on the Jacobean audience who would have expected good to succeed over evil.

Elision

Within the structure of the play there is the use of elision. Elision means that an action happens offstage and the audience does not witness it. The murderous bloodshed in *Macbeth* happens away from the stage. Shakespeare has used the other characters to report what has happened. The purpose of this may be because:

- The bloody murders are very difficult to stage. At the time it was written, Shakespeare had limited stage props and it would have been difficult to show the murders. For example, the slaying of Banquo, or the decapitation of Macbeth.
- The actions are violent and their description by the characters allows the audience to imagine the horror and interpret it in their own way. This could create a more powerful image by leaving it to the audience's imagination.
- The deaths that take place are of kings, women and children. These may have been considered too gruesome and awful for Jacobean audiences to watch, even when they are not real.

The single plot

Macbeth is one of Shakespeare's shortest tragedies. The main reason for this is that there is no sub-plot and the conflict is centred mostly around the character of Macbeth, increasing the intensity of the action which is never really alleviated apart from the very brief scene with the Porter and Macduff. Even within this act there is a constant reference to hell and the devil, and whilst it offers a brief respite from the previous scene and provides some humour, Shakespeare does not allow the audience to relax. The single plot has a powerful effect on the audience and helps to unite the play into a consistent and interconnected whole.

Language

Language is a very important aspect of *Macbeth*. It is interesting to note that many of Shakespeare's phrases are still used today and he uses metaphors and similes* very effectively. The play *Macbeth* uses imagery* to create feelings of foreboding, tension and drama. Shakespeare's use of language is both literal and figurative.

Language used to set the scene

It is important to remember that many of Shakespeare's plays were performed in the open air and even when they were performed inside, the use of props and devices were different from those used today. For example, there was no effective lighting and very few costume or scenery changes. In order to understand the time and place of a scene, it was necessary to use the language as a clue to the time of day, or the weather, or the location. The weather plays a significant part in the mood and tone of this play. This is demonstrated in the first scene when the three witches are discussing when and where they will meet Macbeth:

> "When shall we three meet again?
> In thunder, lightning, or in rain?
> That will be ere the set of sun.
> Where the place?
> Upon the heath."

This gives the audience all they need to set the scene. By setting a scene that focuses on thunder and lightning, the audience is made aware from the outset that the world of *Macbeth* is chaotic and dangerous. They will know from the beginning that this play will have a tragic outcome.

The imagery of blood

Shakespeare's use of 'blood' as a motif occurs over and over in the play. The word "blood" appears in the first act and significantly, it is used by Lady Macbeth and Macbeth to describe their guilt. At the murder of Duncan, Macbeth asks in despair:

> "Will all great Neptune's ocean wash this blood
> Clean from my hand?" [Act 2 Scene 2]

This image of blood represents the overwhelming feeling of guilt that Macbeth feels after what he has done and symbolises that this cannot simply be washed away by water. The blood stains will remain even after his hands have been washed.

The motif continues throughout the rest of the play. After the ghost of Banquo enters the banquet, Macbeth declares: "It will have blood they say: blood will have blood" [Act 3 Scene 4]. Lady Macbeth also dwells on blood when she is sleepwalking and utters the words: "Out damned spot, Out I say" [Act 5 Scene 1]. Like Macbeth in earlier scenes, Lady Macbeth has finally realised that she can no longer wash her hands clean of what she has done and she sees blood on her hands long after they have been washed.

The motif of sleep

Another motif used by Shakespeare as a frequent symbol of guilt is the use of the word 'sleep'. Sleep is recurrent in the play; Duncan has been murdered by Macbeth in his sleep and Macbeth realises that his guilt may prevent him from sleeping ever again:

> "Methought I heard a voice cry, 'sleep no more!'
> Macbeth does murder sleep, the innocent sleep,
> Sleep that knits up the ravell'd sleave of care." [Act 2 Scene 2]

By committing murder, Macbeth has murdered the innocent sleep that is needed to maintain life. Shakespeare uses Macbeth's name for emphasis, to add guilt, and, through his guilt, he will not be able to sleep innocently again.

The motif of sleep appears again in Act 5 Scene 1 when Lady Macbeth's sleep is disrupted by her guilt and the doctor describes how she now sleepwalks. Like Macbeth, her guilt has disturbed her "innocent sleep" and she cannot rest easy because of what she has done.

Imagery

Imagery and vivid descriptions are used frequently by Shakespeare in *Macbeth* to give more depth to an action or character. Imagery can take the form of metaphor or simile or personification. For example, the imagery of birds plays an important part in the play. Lady Macbeth speaks of the "raven" in Act 1 Scene 5, which is a bird associated with death. The fact that it "croaks the fatal entrance" of Duncan foreshadows that he will die in the castle that night. Also, at the death of King Duncan in Act 2 Scene 2, she says she heard "It was the owl that shrieked". In Jacobean times, an owl flying over someone's house meant that death would visit the household. This again signals the death of Duncan.

As well as birds, there are references made to other animals. For example, Macbeth refers to scorpions as animals which plague his mind in Act 3 Scene 2: "O full of scorpions is my mind, dear wife". This metaphorical use of scorpions explains how Macbeth's mind is full of guilt and fear. Furthermore, when the witches make up their magic spell, body parts of different animals go into the cauldron including:

> "Eye of newt, and toe of frog,
> Wool of bat and tongue of dog,
> Adder's fork and blind-worm's sting"

These animals are all associated with the idea of the supernatural and witchcraft. They were used by Shakespeare as the audience may have been familiar with them as evil or dangerous.

Blank verse

Blank verse does not rhyme but has stresses on certain syllables which mimic natural speech. This was the preferred form of writing in the sixteenth and the early seventeenth century and most plays were written in this style. In *Macbeth* blank verse is spoken by all of the characters most of the time, with the exception of the witches.

Rhyming couplets

The witches use rhyme rather than blank verse. This is often in the form of rhyming couplets. Rhyming couplets are pairs of lines where the end word in the line rhymes with the next end word. The witches are the only ones that consistently speak in rhyme, which adds to the strangeness of their speech and confirms their supernatural powers. Shakespeare uses this difference in speech for a specific purpose. It separates the witches from other characters and gives them a sense of "otherness". Their spells and incantations take on a 'chant-like' quality. The other characters speak in what can be considered natural speech. It is important to recognise the witches are not human, they are supernatural beings and the rhyming couplets help to emphasise this.

Progress and Revision Check

1. How does the structure of the play follow the life of Macbeth?
2. What is elision?
3. How did Shakespeare manage the lack of scenery and lighting?
4. What effect does a single plot have on an audience?
5. What is the meaning of a motif?
6. Why does Shakespeare use the imagery of birds?
7. What is meant by blank verse and how is it used in the play?
8. What is the significance of the witches speaking in rhyme?
9. What is meant by the form of the play and what are the key features of this form?
10. What do the motifs of blood and sleep represent?

~ KEY QUOTATIONS AND GLOSSARY ~

Key Quotations

CHARACTER	ACT / SCENE	QUOTATION	EXPLANATION
Captain	Act 1 Scene 2	"For brave Macbeth– well he deserves that name– / Disdaining Fortune, with his brandish'd steel, / Which smoked with bloody execution."	The Captain is describing Macbeth's bravery in the battle to King Duncan.
Macbeth	Act 1 Scene 5	"My dearest partner"	Macbeth is speaking about his wife, demonstrating his love for her.
Macbeth	Act 1 Scene 7	"I have no spur / To prick the sides of my intent, but only / Vaulting ambition, which o'erleaps itself / And falls on th' other."	Macbeth admits his only motive for killing Duncan is his ambition.
Macbeth	Act 1 Scene 7	"We will proceed no further with this business."	Macbeth has decided not to murder King Duncan.
Macbeth	Act 3 Scene 5	"It will have blood they say: blood will have blood."	Macbeth is referring to the murder of Banquo and believes that one murder will lead to another.
Macbeth	Act 5 Scene 5	"Tomorrow, and tomorrow, and tomorrow / Creeps in this petty pace from day to day"	Macbeth is contemplating thoughts of death and the pointlessness of living.
Macbeth	Act 5 Scene 8	"I throw my war-like shield. Lay on, Macduff, / And damn'd be he that first cries, 'Hold, enough!'"	Macbeth's valiant and final act of bravery in fighting Macduff.

Lady Macbeth	Act 1 Scene 5	"Come, you spirits / That tend on mortal thoughts! Unsex me here, / And fill me from the crown to the toe top full / Of direst cruelty;"	Lady Macbeth is appealing to the spirits to change her femininity and replace it with cruelty.
Lady Macbeth	Act 1 Scene 5	"Look like the innocent flower, but be the serpent under't."	Lady Macbeth tells Macbeth to act innocently in front of the King to deceive him.
Lady Macbeth	Act 1 Scene 5	"Yet do I fear thy nature; / It is too full o' the milk of human kindness."	Lady Macbeth is fully aware of Macbeth's kind character.
Lady Macbeth	Act 5 Scene 1	"Yet who would have thought the old man to have so much blood in him?"	Lady Macbeth is reflecting on the murder of King Duncan.
Lady Macbeth	Act 5 Scene 1	"What will these hands ne'er be clean?"	Lady Macbeth reflects on the metaphorical blood on her hands.
Witches	Act 1 Scene 3	"All hail Macbeth, hail to thee, Thane of Glamis." "All hail Macbeth, hail to thee, Thane of Cawdor." "All hail Macbeth, that shalt be King hereafter."	The witches greet Macbeth with the three prophecies, which arouses his ambition.
Witches	Act 1 Scene 1	"Fair is foul, and foul is fair"	The witches' attitude to life. This is a contradiction where nothing is what it seems.
Witches	Act 4 Scene 1	"Double, double toil and trouble: / Fire burn, and cauldron bubble."	The witches prepare for Macbeth, chanting these words as they make a spell to bewitch him.
Witches	Act 4 Scene 1	"By the pricking of my thumbs, / Something wicked this way comes."	This is a reference to Macbeth as something 'wicked'. The witches have changed Macbeth's character by their meddling.

~ Key Quotations and Glossary ~

Banquo	Act 3 Scene 1	"Thou hast it now: King, Cawdor, Glamis, all, / As the weird women promised, and I fear / Thou play'dst most foully for't."	Banquo reflects on Macbeth and the way he has risen to become King; Banquo is suspicious but says nothing.
Banquo	Act 2 Scene 3	"Look to the lady"	Even though Banquo is horrified at the sight of the murdered King Duncan, he still shows chivalry towards Lady Macbeth.
Macduff	Act 4 Scene 3	"All my pretty ones? / Did you say all? O hell-kite! All? / What, all my pretty chickens and their dam / At one fell swoop?"	Macduff hears that his family have been murdered by Macbeth. He is so shocked he cannot believe what he hears.
Macduff	Act 5 Scene 8	"Macduff was from his mother's womb / Untimely ripp'd."	Macduff informs Macbeth the he was not naturally born of woman and was born by caesarean section.
Malcolm	Act 5 Scene 9	"Of this dead butcher and his fiend like queen"	Malcolm's describes Macbeth and Lady Macbeth.

~ Key Quotations and Glossary ~

Glossary

Anti-Catholic means to go against the Catholic religion and the word of the Clergy.

Caesarean Section is an operation for delivering a child by cutting through the wall of the mother's abdomen.

Chronicles of Scotland was written by Raphael Holinshed. It was mostly based on real events. Shakespeare used Holinshed's work extensively in *Macbeth*, but he deliberately changed the characters to give the play more drama.

Doctrine is a set of guidelines which must be followed.

Dramatic Irony is a literary technique where the significance of a character's words is clear to the audience but are not realised by the character themselves.

Imagery is where a writer carefully chooses words and phrases to create "mental images" for the reader.

Irony refers to the use of words to convey a meaning where something that is intended has the opposite effect. It can also be used as a sarcastic or humorous expression.

Metaphor is a figure of speech that makes an unspoken, indirect, or hidden comparison between two things that are unrelated, but which share some common characteristics.

Phenomenon is something or someone who is remarkable or amazing.

Protestantism is the religion or religious system of any of the Churches that preach Christianity but not the religion of Catholicism.

Regicide is someone who kills or takes part in killing a king.

Simile is where a parallel or a comparison is made between two unrelated things, people or places. Similes are marked by the words 'like', 'as', or 'such as'.

Symbol is an object that represents or stands for something else.

Tragic Hero is someone who faces danger or demonstrates courage, such as Macbeth's bravery in the war, but who faces a downfall through their own actions.

~ Revision and Exam Help ~

Exam Preparation

Your best preparation for the exam is to get to know the play as well as you can. This does not mean just the plot, but ALL the analysis, characters, themes, form, structure and language that are covered in this guide. However, in order to do this to the best of your ability, you need to know what the exam is testing you on.

Assessment objectives

Assessment objectives simply means "what you are being tested on". The exam will assess you on four main skills:

Assessment Objective	What It Says	What It Means
AO1	Read, understand and respond to texts Students should be able to: • maintain a critical style and develop an informed personal response • use textual references, including quotations, to support and illustrate interpretations	• This is checking if you have understood the main elements of the **plot, characters, themes and relationships** in the text. • You need to create **arguments based on your personal opinions** of the characters, themes and relationships. • You need to use **quotations and examples** that prove the arguments you are making.
AO2	Analyse the language, form and structure used by a writer to create meanings and effects, using relevant subject terminology where appropriate	• You need to back up the arguments you are making by analysing **how language, form and structure help to prove your point**. • You need to analyse **the writer's purpose or intention when using these techniques** and what they are trying to make the audience think, learn or feel. • You need to use **the correct terms** when identifying language, form and structure.

AO3	*Show understanding of the relationships between texts and the contexts in which they were written*	• You need to explain **how the writer was influenced** by the following during the time that the text was written: - What was happening **in society and politics** - What was happening **in literature** - What was happening to **the playwright personally.**
AO4	*Use a range of vocabulary and sentence structures for clarity, purpose and effect, with accurate spelling and punctuation*	• This checks that you are using: wide-ranging and ambitious vocabulary; simple, compound and complex sentences correctly; and that your spelling and punctuation, are accurate. • 5% of the marks in English Literature are for spelling, grammar and punctuation so make sure you proof-read your work to get these marks.

Mapping your revision – The "Journey"

Every character, theme and relationship goes on *a journey* through the play; this is not a physical journey, but what this means is that they will either change, grow or develop from the beginning to the end of the play. For a clear way to revise, follow these steps:

1. Choose a character, theme or relationship to revise. The sub-headings in this guide are a great place to start. Now find the important pages for your chosen area of revision in this guide. As an example, the character of Macbeth is completed below.

2. Write down what you think the writer's overall purpose is for this character/ theme/relationship using the information you read in the guide. For example: *"Shakespeare's purpose for Macbeth was to demonstrate the terrible results of a weak male character who is driven solely by ambition."*

3. The first question that you should ask yourself is: *"How does the character/ theme/relationship change, grow or develop during the text?"* Now, plot these on an arrow that represents the beginning to the end. Choose what you think are the top five key moments:

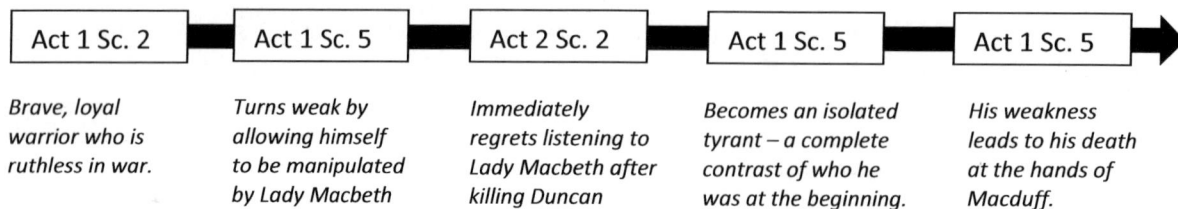

Act 1 Sc. 2	Act 1 Sc. 5	Act 2 Sc. 2	Act 1 Sc. 5	Act 1 Sc. 5
Brave, loyal warrior who is ruthless in war.	*Turns weak by allowing himself to be manipulated by Lady Macbeth*	*Immediately regrets listening to Lady Macbeth after killing Duncan*	*Becomes an isolated tyrant – a complete contrast of who he was at the beginning.*	*His weakness leads to his death at the hands of Macduff.*

4. Choose key quotations that are the **best** example of what you have said about the character/theme/relationship. For example:

> Act 2 Sc. 2

*Immediately regrets listening to
Lady Macbeth after killing Duncan.*

⬇

"will all great Neptune's ocean wash this blood clean from my hand?"

5. Analyse the language, form or structure of your chosen quotation. You could also choose to discuss the importance of where this scene appears in the text. For example:

"will all great Neptune's ocean wash this blood clean from my hand?"

⬇

*Rhetorical Question and Exaggeration: He believes nothing can
wash the guilt away that he feels, not even an ocean of water.*

6. Add important contextual information that you think has influenced the writer in making the choices that they have made. You may not need this for every key moment you have chosen. There is also no need to repeat yourself! For example:

> Act 2 Sc. 2

*Immediately regrets listening to Lady
Macbeth after killing Duncan.*

⬇

*Very unusual Jacobean relationship to have the wife in control of
the husband. A Jacobean audience would have found this very
disturbing and would have suggested something evil and
unnatural.*

Once you have done this, you have revised everything that you need to know about the character/theme/relationship, and you have used this revision guide in a really meaningful way. It also means that you should have the information you need to answer an exam question on your chosen area of revision.

Remember: if you know the text well enough, there is NOTHING you can't answer!

The Exam Question

The type of question that you will be asked will depend on what exam board that your school is entering you for. The most popular exam boards that examine *Macbeth* are:

Exam Board	What Paper it will be on	What you will be asked to do in the exam
AQA	Paper 1	There is no choice. Answer one question about a particular character/theme/relationship in the extract and the text as a whole. AO4 is marked in this question.
Edexcel	Paper 1	There is no choice. There are two parts to the question: A and B. Answer Part A on the language, form and structure used to describe a topic in the extract and Part B on a particular character/theme/relationship in the text as a whole.
Eduquas	Component 1	There is no choice. There are two parts to the question: A and B. Answer Part A on a character/theme/relationship evident in the extract and Part B on a particular character/theme/relationship in the text as a whole. AO4 is marked in this question. AO3 is not.
OCR	Component 2	There is a choice of question. The first question asks you about a particular character/theme/relationship in the extract and the text as a whole. The second question has no extract and asks you to analyse a character/theme/relationship throughout the play. AO4 is marked in this question.

Remember: it is important to know which exam board you are studying!
Double check with your teacher so that you revise correctly.

Answering the question

1. Read the question twice so that you fully understand what it is asking you to do.

2. Underline the character/theme/relationship that you are being asked to answer on. This will be the focus of your answer. Underline any other key words and phrases that are important.

   Hint: every year the wording of the question will stay the same. The only thing that will change will be the focus of the question; the changing words are what you should be underlining as this will tell you exactly what you need to answer on.

3. If you are asked to answer on an extract, read it through twice. The first time, just read it through so you understand what is happening. The second time, underline important words or phrases that will help you to answer the question.

> How does Shakespeare present Macbeth as a weak character in the play? Refer to the following extract in your answer.

Your focus is on Macbeth, specifically about your opinion about whether he is weak or not.

Important exam question language

Exam questions are worded in a similar way every year. This is why it is important that you know exactly what they mean.

Key Word	What it means
Explore/Explain	This means that you should make three or four points about the character, theme or relationship so that you have gone into enough detail.
Attitudes to	You are being asked to discuss the way a character/lots of characters think and feel about a particular theme, which may show in the way they behave towards something.
How Shakespeare uses	"How" asks you to look at Shakespeare's techniques, such as the language, form and structure of the text to support the arguments you have made.
How far you agree	You will have been given a statement and you can choose to agree or disagree (or both!) with this statement, using evidence from the text.
Refer to	This means what you should mention specifically in your answer.

Planning Your Answer

This is one of the most important parts of what you will do in the exam! The majority of the marks you get are based on whether you develop your argument and you cannot do that if you haven't planned. It will also help you feel calm and less overwhelmed in the exam. Planning also helps you to choose the best ideas that match your argument, rather than the first one that comes to your head.

The step-by-step approach to the five-minute plan

1. Brainstorm or bullet point everything you remember about the character, theme or relationship you have been asked about. Empty your head! This should take no longer than thirty seconds. Make sure you include at least one idea from the extract if you have been given one.

2. Write down the numbers 1-5 on your planning sheet, leaving space to jot your ideas down. This will be the basic structure of your answer. This is what you should write beside each number:

   1: Write a summary of the journey that the character, theme or relationship takes during the play. Just write one or two sentences.

   *2-4: Use your brainstorming from Step 1 to choose the three key moments in the text that demonstrate the argument you created. You will have loads in your brainstorm, but you must now choose **the best ideas**. Remember, if there is an extract, make sure to include at least one idea from the extract.*

   5: Sum up your main point and write down what you think the playwright's purpose was for creating the character, theme or relationship like this.

3. Go back over your plan and include the best quotes for 2-4. You do not need any additional quotes in your introduction or conclusion.

4. Read over your plan. Add any context or language techniques that you remember from your revision. This way, when you use your plan to write your answer, you won't forget to add this important information. You might also want to juggle around the paragraphs if you think they would work better in another order.

Language analysis is included using the correct term (Step 4)

Key moment from Act 1 (Step 2)

Example plan for how Macbeth is presented in *Macbeth*

1. Macbeth – outlines the tragic downfall of a heroic, loyal warrior whose ambition causes him to betray his King, which causes his downfall.

2. Beginning: a brave, loyal warrior at the beginning, who defends his King ruthlessly. Very violent images of his actions: "unseam'd him from the nave to th'chaps". He is introduced by others to show the strength of his reputation but his vicious nature might foreshadow his brutality later.

3. Changes when he is manipulated by Lady Macbeth and immediately regrets listening to her after killing Duncan: "will all great Neptune's ocean wash this blood clean from my hand?" Very unusual Jacobean relationship to have the wife in control of the husband. A Jacobean audience would have found this very disturbing and would have suggested something evil and unnatural.

Best quote to show his change (Step 3)

4. His death at the end at the hands of Macduff: symmetrical structure where the traitor of the King (Macbeth) has been killed by a loyal and brave warrior – shows the dangers of ambition and going against the will of God.

5. Shakespeare's purpose for Macbeth was to demonstrate the terrible results of a weak male character who is driven solely by ambition.

Golden Rules of Planning

1. Only give yourself five minutes at the beginning of each question. The plan itself doesn't get any marks so any longer will just eat into your essay-writing time.

2. Look back at your plan before you write a paragraph. This will keep you on track and will make sure you don't forget anything you want to say.

3. Use a full page to plan out your response. You don't have to worry about running out of space in your exam booklet; you can always ask for more paper.

Writing Introductions

Your introduction is the first impression you will make on an examiner, so it is important that it has an impact to get you the grade you deserve.

Your introduction is Step 1 from your plan, which you will now develop:

1: Write a summary of the journey that the character, theme or relationship takes during the text.

- Make sure that you answer the question in detail, talking about how the character, theme or relationship changes, grows or develops from the beginning to the end.
- Make sure that the points of the question that you talk about are what is on your plan – your examiner will then have a really clear idea what you are going to talk about.
- Explain the playwright's purpose for this character, theme or relationship. What message are they trying to get across to their audiences by including this?
- You could start by using words from the question in your introduction to help you begin.

Example Introduction: Explore how the character of Macbeth is presented in *Macbeth*

In the play Macbeth, through the main character, Shakespeare outlines the tragic downfall of a heroic, loyal warrior whose ambition causes him to betray his King, which causes his downfall. His drastic change from loyalty to betrayal happens in a shocking manner, resulting in the death of the main character because of the acts he has carried out. Perhaps Shakespeare is warning his audience of the dangers of uncontrolled ambition in man and the dangers of the influences of women.

Writing Main Paragraphs

This is the section where you are going to get the bulk of your marks. This is the opportunity for you to expand on what you have said in your introduction and really develop your arguments.

Your main paragraphs are Steps 2-4 of your plan, which you will now develop:

> **2-4:** *Use your brainstorming from Step 1 to choose the three key moments in the text that demonstrate the argument you have created. You will have loads in your brainstorm, but you must now choose **the best ideas**. Remember, if there is an extract, make sure to include at least 1 idea from the extract.*

Paragraph structure

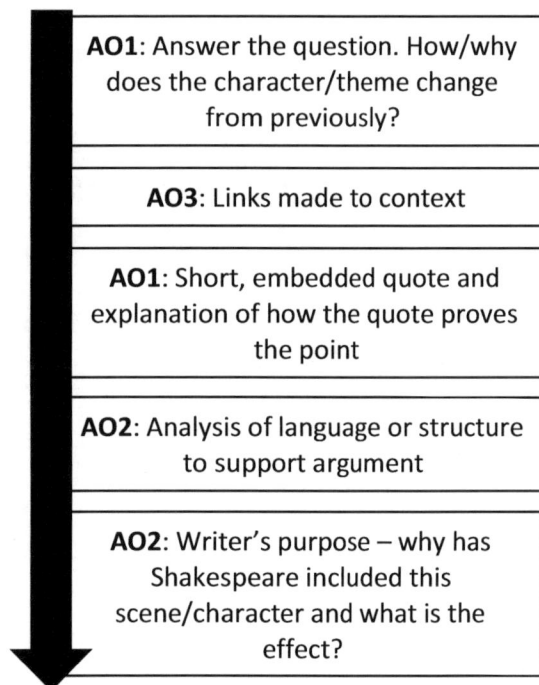

AO1: Answer the question. How/why does the character/theme change from previously?

AO3: Links made to context

AO1: Short, embedded quote and explanation of how the quote proves the point

AO2: Analysis of language or structure to support argument

AO2: Writer's purpose – why has Shakespeare included this scene/character and what is the effect?

The paragraph structure to the left will help you to develop your argument fully to make sure that you meet all of the assessment objectives.

AO1: Your argument and opinions and your ability to back up your arguments with evidence from the text.

AO2: Your analysis of language and structure, as well as your explanation of why the writer made the decisions they did.

AO3: Your explanation of how the text links to the context. This is done best when it is linked to your argument.

Example main paragraph: Explore how the character of Macbeth is presented in *Macbeth (argument from Act 5)*

AO1: argument	*Finally, in Act 5 Scene 8, Shakespeare dramatises Macbeth's downfall as a direct result of the witches' influence over him. The audience witness a man who is still fighting to defend his behaviour to the end in a remorseless manner; he is unrepentant for all of the hurt he has caused. Macbeth has completely gone against the code of conduct of a thane by killing the innocent and therefore, in this scene, a Jacobean audience will be waiting for his punishment. Macbeth's final lines depict how he "will try the last" and "throw my warlike shield" before his body, symbolising that he is willing to fight until the bitter end and not accept all the wrongdoings that he has done. It is significant that the image of Macbeth in this scene is again one of violence, just like it was in Act 1 Scene 2 when he fought the traitors of Duncan. This is specifically and deliberately done by Shakespeare to reinforce the fact that he is also a traitor of the King and must suffer the most severe consequence – death. The audience is left with a feeling that justice has been carried out when Macbeth dies as he has refused to admit his wrongdoings and has allowed himself to fall victim to the control of the supernatural. Shakespeare is demonstrating, in the most extreme way, the deadly consequences of ambition to a man.*
AO3: context linked	
AO1: quotation	
AO2: language analysis	
AO2: writer's purpose	

Dos and don'ts when writing main paragraphs

DO

- Link your paragraphs together to create a "flow" in your essay. Refer back to what you said previously.
- Write more than one sentence for each part of the paragraph structure. Explain yourself fully!
- Give more than one interpretation of language/structure if you can, and only if it links to the argument you are making.
- Make sure that every part of the structure refers back to the first sentence and your overall argument.

DON'T

- Repeat context that you have said before. It is not necessary to put context in every paragraph if it means you are just repeating yourself.
- Use the same sentence starters for all three paragraphs. Your writing will sound like you are filling in the blanks!
- Forget to always say "why". Why has the character changed? Why has the writer used that language technique? Why does that quotation prove your point?

Writing Conclusions

If your introduction is your first impression, then the conclusion is the last impression you give the examiner before they award you a mark. That's why it needs to be punchy, impactful and meaningful!

Your conclusion is Step 5 from your plan, which you will now develop:

> **5:** *Sum up your main point and write down what you think the playwright's purpose was for creating the character, theme or relationship like this.*

- Make sure that you summarise the journey that the character or theme has been on in one or two sentences.
- Explain the writer's overall purpose for this character, theme or relationship. What is the big message that they are trying to get across?
- Don't introduce any new ideas – this is your opportunity to summarise your key arguments.

Example Conclusion:
Explore how the character of Macbeth is presented in *Macbeth*

In conclusion, Shakespeare reveals a fully changed character to his audience by the end of Act 5. Macbeth has undergone such a dramatic change that he is now the complete opposite of the Macbeth we meet in Act 1 and a Jacobean audience would have felt that he rightly deserved to die. Shakespeare's purpose for Macbeth in the play as a whole was to demonstrate the terrible results of a weak male character who is driven solely by ambition.

Using Quotations in the Exam

The whole point of having quotations in your response is to prove the arguments that you make. However, that doesn't mean you have to learn the whole play off by heart!

Tips and tricks for using quotations:

1. Look at the key quotations on page 60 of this revision guide.
2. Choose the quotations that **best** prove the point you are trying to make about the character, theme or relationship.
3. Keep your quotations to a couple of words or a phrase. Don't write long amounts of text into your answer. Just stick to the part that actually proves what you are saying.
4. Try to embed your quotations into the sentence rather than saying: "this can be seen in the quote". This simply means making the quotations part of your own sentence.
5. Always use quotation marks!

Not embedded:
Shakespeare describes how Macbeth intended to act when he meets Macduff. This can be seen in the quote: "Yet I will try the last. Before my body, I throw my warlike shield".

Embedded:
Macbeth's final lines depict how he "will try the last" and "throw my warlike shield" before his body.

Here is another example:

Not embedded:
In Act 1 Shakespeare presents Macbeth as a ruthless warrior who is very vicious in war. This can be seen in the quote: "unseam'd him from the nave to th'chaps".

Embedded:
In Act 1, Shakespeare presents Macbeth as a ruthless warrior who "unseam'd" the traitor "from the nave to th'chaps", demonstrating the extent of the violence that he showed to those who were disloyal.

It may seem like only a small change to embed the quote, but it will help the examiner to follow what you are saying more easily and will make your paragraph "flow".

Improving Your Written Expression

AO1, the first assessment objective, talks about the "style" of your writing. It must be formal and critical, meaning that it should feel balanced and not too over-the-top.

Sentence starters to avoid and sophisticated substitutions

When you use the same sentence starters and phrases in an essay, it can feel stiff and unnatural to read. These are some simple changes you can make so that your essay sounds more formal and will help you to vary your response:

Avoid overusing...	Use instead...
"Shakespeare **presents** Macbeth as..."	• Shakespeare **illustrates** Macbeth as... • Shakespeare **portrays** Macbeth as... • Shakespeare **depicts** Macbeth as... • Shakespeare **reveals** Macbeth as...to the audience • Shakespeare **paints** Macbeth as...
"This **shows...**"	• This **suggests**... • This **indicates**... • This **implies** ... • This **infers**...
"I think/I feel/I believe..." *(never use "I" in an essay)*	• It could be argued that... • The audience is left with the impression that... • The audience is positioned to feel that... • This could be interpreted as...
"The character **represents...**"	• The character **symbolises**... • The character **embodies**... • The character **reflects**... • The character **epitomises**... • The character **typifies**... • The character **exemplifies**...

Joining ideas and paragraphs together

If you start every single paragraph with the same word or in the same way, then it will get boring for the examiner.

1. Use adding and contrasting connectives to make connections between your paragraphs and improve the fluency of your writing.

   Adding connectives: 'In addition', 'Moreover', 'Furthermore', 'Similarly', 'As well as', 'Consequently'

   Contrasting connectives: 'In contrast', 'However', 'Alternatively', 'On the other hand', 'Whereas'.

2. Add signposts for the examiner at the beginning of your paragraphs to let them know the part of the text you will be talking about.

   Signposts: 'At the beginning of the play', 'Later on, in Act 3', 'Finally', 'Eventually', 'In conclusion'.

Using Evaluative Adjectives

Just like in English Language, you may wish to make a judgement about how successful the playwright has been in achieving their purpose. This is another way of achieving the "critical style" that AO1 sets out. You could do this by using the following adjectives:

Adjective	Example
Skilful/Skilfully	*Shakespeare **skilfully** uses the character of Macbeth to…*
Subtle/Subtly	*The use of …is a **subtle** hint that…*
Pivotal	*This **pivotal** moment in the play means the audience is positioned to feel…*
Effective	*This is an **effective** method employed by Shakespeare to…*
Striking	*This **striking** image serves to…*
Challenging	*This is a **challenging** moment in the play that allows the audience to…*
Central concern	*The theme of … is a **central concern** to the play.*
Significant	*This is particularly **significant** because…*

Some further sophisticated analytical tips:

1. Analysing an alternative interpretation
   - *The phrase could also be interpreted as revealing…*

2. Analysing the combined effect of several techniques together
   - *The writer uses _____ coupled with_____ to illustrate…*

3. Tracking how key ideas are developed through a text
   - *This idea is further developed when…*

4. Deepening the analysis of a character/theme
   - *On the exterior _____, yet on further inspection of the character the audience sees…*
   - *At first glance _____; however, on closer inspection the audience learns…*

Making the main paragraph even more analytical

Let's look back at the example main paragraph from earlier and see all of these written expressions in action:

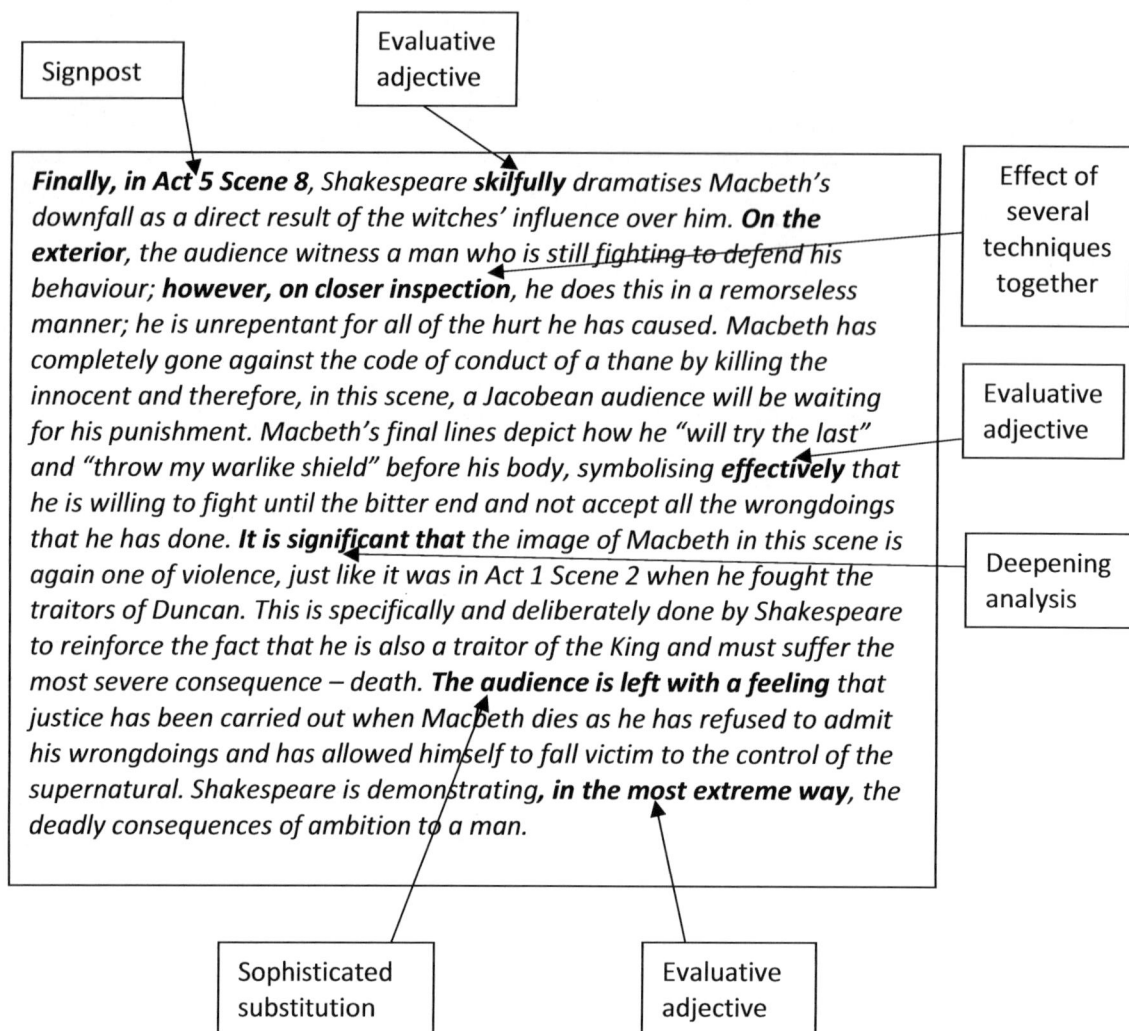

| Signpost | | Evaluative adjective |

Finally, in Act 5 Scene 8, Shakespeare **skilfully** dramatises Macbeth's downfall as a direct result of the witches' influence over him. **On the exterior**, the audience witness a man who is still fighting to defend his behaviour; **however, on closer inspection**, he does this in a remorseless manner; he is unrepentant for all of the hurt he has caused. Macbeth has completely gone against the code of conduct of a thane by killing the innocent and therefore, in this scene, a Jacobean audience will be waiting for his punishment. Macbeth's final lines depict how he "will try the last" and "throw my warlike shield" before his body, symbolising **effectively** that he is willing to fight until the bitter end and not accept all the wrongdoings that he has done. **It is significant that** the image of Macbeth in this scene is again one of violence, just like it was in Act 1 Scene 2 when he fought the traitors of Duncan. This is specifically and deliberately done by Shakespeare to reinforce the fact that he is also a traitor of the King and must suffer the most severe consequence – death. **The audience is left with a feeling** that justice has been carried out when Macbeth dies as he has refused to admit his wrongdoings and has allowed himself to fall victim to the control of the supernatural. Shakespeare is demonstrating**, in the most extreme way,** the deadly consequences of ambition to a man.

Effect of several techniques together

Evaluative adjective

Deepening analysis

Sophisticated substitution

Evaluative adjective

~ PROGRESS AND REVISION CHECK ANSWERS ~

Background Information

1. Travelling players often visited Stratford-upon-Avon and may have helped Shakespeare decide to become a playwright.
2. Shakespeare wrote comedies, tragedies and historical plays.
3. The source of *Macbeth* was found in 'The Chronicles of Scotland' by Raphael Holinshed.
4. Macbeth needed to adapt the original story because it showed that some of James 1st ancestors were murderers. Also, Shakespeare wanted to show the dangers of believing in witchcraft.
5. Women were expected to obey their fathers, brothers and husbands. It was expected that well-to-do women must show their respect and to act in a feminine manner.
6. The main event in 1605 was the Gunpowder Plot, which failed but nevertheless caused fear and suspicion in King James, who turned against the Catholics.
7. The main religion in England at this time was Protestantism.
8. In the time of Shakespeare, religion formed the teaching of the people. People believed that what happened in this world determined their position in the next world.
9. The Divine Right of Kings meant that the King became God's representative on earth. The King's judgement was final. Opposing the King was going against the rule of God and dreadful consequences would follow.
10. Shakespeare created Lady Macbeth as a dangerous woman to persuade supporters of Queen Elizabeth that a man should be on the throne rather than a woman.

The Play – A Summary

1. Macbeth is shocked by the prophecies of the witches but, unlike Banquo, he believes them to be true and invests in them at great cost. Banquo is more amused by the witches' predictions.
2. Lady Macbeth is delighted by the news and immediately makes plans for Macbeth to commit murder.
3. Macbeth considers what he is about to do and feels strongly that he should not go through with the murder. Macbeth feels that it is his duty to be loyal and faithful to his King and, as his thane, protect him.
4. Macduff discovers that the King has been horribly murdered and becomes almost hysterical when he alerts the other characters.
5. Macbeth immediately kills the King's guards after his initial reaction of horror. This immediate slaying of the guards adds to the suspicion felt by Macduff.

6. Banquo is murdered by a group of Macbeth's henchmen who were following the orders of Macbeth.
7. The witches warn Macbeth to be wary of Macduff and this is sufficient for Macbeth to feel threatened by him.
8. Macbeth sees three apparitions, the first is an armed head, who tells Macbeth to beware of Macduff. The second apparition appears as a bloody child who explains that none of woman born shall harm Macbeth. The third apparition is that of a child crowned with a tree in his hand.
9. Macbeth realises that he has been deceived by the witches at the end of the play, when Macduff explains he was born by caesarean section and was not born naturally.
10. The ending of the play is a fitting conclusion as it brings the downfall and death of Macbeth whilst serving as justice for the revenge of his wrongdoings.

Characters

1. Macbeth is presented as brave and loyal. He has served his King well by slaying the enemy. He is also a loving husband to Lady Macbeth.
2. Macbeth immediately reacts to the witches by taking their predictions as a true reflection of what is to happen. He sees them as truths rather than fiction.
3. Lady Macbeth uses powerful, insulting and persuasive language to force Macbeth into action, and this may show how easily his character can be manipulated.
4. At the end of the play Macbeth's character has dramatically changed and becomes a figure of hate. He is feared by the people of Scotland because he is a tyrant.
5. Lady Macbeth realises the failings of herself as an ordinary woman and asks the spirits of the supernatural world to change these characteristics to make her strong and determined.
6. The witches are presented as supernatural beings who are evil. The witches represent evil and fear. Their influence has a great effect on Macbeth.
7. Banquo is cautious and perhaps more rational then Macbeth. He appears to be less gullible than Macbeth and he is clearly rational in his thoughts.
8. A Jacobean audience would be shocked and horrified by the murder of Macduff's family, especially the murder of Macduff's son, as women and children were considered innocent.
9. Macduff feels hatred and is full of revenge. His plan is to challenge Macbeth and ultimately kill him.
10. Macbeth reverts to his natural characteristics of bravery as he feels life has become worthless and his ambitions have come to nothing.

Themes

1. Macbeth's ambition is awakened by the witches' prophecies and he becomes obsessed by their predictions.
2. Lady Macbeth's ambition is established in the play by her calling on the spirits of the supernatural to change her personality so that she can use her powers of persuasion over Macbeth.
3. The witches' prophecies may suggest to Macbeth a different future to the one laid out for him. It may be considered that his fate is completely responsible for his downfall.
4. The weather is described as chaotic and wet with strong winds, which suggest a threatening feeling to the play.
5. The ghost of Banquo is important as it is seen as a representation of the supernatural but can only be seen by Macbeth, which highlights the magic of the witches.
6. Macduff must take revenge on Macbeth. It is expected because of his position as a thane, as well as the fact that Macbeth has murdered his family. It is completely understandable for Macduff to want to take revenge on Macbeth.
7. Revenge in the time of Shakespeare was a natural form of justice and it was seen as the right thing to do. Revenge, nowadays may not be an acceptable action.
8. Shakespeare needed to show how ruthless evil can be and the violence and brutality of Macbeth's reign reinforces this idea.
9. The main qualities of a king was to be fair, and loyal to his people, to show kindness but above all goodness. The King is God's representative on earth and is fair and just, but has the power to change and make decisions.
10. The idea of kingship is important to the play. Macbeth did not have any of the qualities of a good king and the audience would understand how dangerous a ruler such as Macbeth would be for the country.

Form, Structure and Language

1. The structure of the play follows the life of Macbeth in a chronological order from his first meeting with the witches to his final defeat by Macduff.
2. Elision is when a particular action takes place offstage and the audience do not watch it. For example, the deaths of King Duncan and Lady Macbeth.
3. Shakespeare managed the lack of scenery and lighting by ensuring that the characters speak lines which give information regarding the time of day, or the weather. This gave the audience the clues they needed to understand what was taking place and where.
4. The use of a single plot has the effect of being able to hold the audience's attention and to reinforce the single idea that the play is about the greatness and downfall of Macbeth.
5. A motif is an idea that is repeated throughout the play to add emphasis and

allow the audience to focus on certain ideas.

6. Birds are used by Shakespeare to foreshadow evil, such as the raven and the owl. Jacobean audiences would have understood the symbolism of these birds.

7. Blank verse was a style of writing which was closer to natural speech than other forms of rhyme. It is used in the play to show the difference between and the witches and the other characters.

8. The significance of the witches speaking in rhyme is to show that they are not of the human world but are supernatural. The rhyme helps to give the witches a chant-like rhythm which is appropriate for their prophecies and spells.

9. The form is that of a tragedy. The classic tragedy followed the protagonist who had to be someone of importance, who displays a fatal flaw in their character and their fatal flaw causes both their downfall and their death.

10. Both the motifs of sleep and blood represent the guilt that Macbeth and Lady Macbeth feel for their part in the death of King Duncan.

Printed in Great Britain
by Amazon